Praise for
Beat the Incumbent

"A thoughtful compendium of campaign advice, combining theory and practice, authored by a consultant whose political experience is both deep and broad. If you are running, or helping a candidate run, or just want to understand political campaigns, you should be reading this very helpful book. If you're a serious campaigner, the pages will soon be dog-eared, as you'll find yourself referring to it often."

—Mark Mellman,
pollster, strategist, and Hall of Fame member of the American Association of Political Consultants

"If candidates follow Dr. Louis Perron's advice on the importance of a central compelling message, it could make the difference between victory and defeat. The importance of a succinct raison d'être cannot be overemphasized."

—Carlton Ballowe,
chairman of the Republican Committee, Nelson County, Virginia

"Dr. Perron is the ultimate expert in winning elections. If you're serious about running, read this book."

—Andrea Römmele,
dean and professor at the Hertie School, Berlin

"Louis Perron combines analytical ability with a hands-on campaign approach. His book provides a rare transnational insight into the world of campaigning. Candidates, practitioners, and academics will love it."

—Dr. Thomas Hofer,
political analyst, Vienna

"*Beat the Incumbent* is a compelling guide for political experts and candidates that offers an insightful blend of scholarly research and practical experience. Louis Perron provides a promising model and campaigning strategies adaptable to various political contexts."

—Romain Lachat,
associate professor at Centre for
Political Research at Sciences Po, Paris

"With fascinating real-world examples, *Beat the Incumbent* provides hands-on advice for political candidates based on Louis Perron's many years as a political consultant. He tells you in a refreshingly open and direct manner how to win elections as a political challenger. Even if you are not running for office, you will learn an immense amount about how electoral campaigning works in contemporary democracies."

—Hanspeter Kriesi,
professor at European University Institute, Florence

BEAT *the* INCUMBENT

PROVEN STRATEGIES AND TACTICS TO WIN ELECTIONS

LOUIS PERRON, PhD

Radius Book Group
New York

Radius Book Group
A Division of Diversion Publishing Corp.
www.RadiusBookGroup.com

For more information, email info@radiusbookgroup.com.

First edition: January 2024
Hardcover ISBN: 978-1-63576-840-4
eBook ISBN: 978-1-63576-847-3

Manufactured in the United States of America

10 9 8 7 6 5 4 3 2 1

Cover design by Jen Huppert
Interior design by Neuwirth & Associates, Inc.

Radius Book Group and the Radius Book Group colophon
are registered trademarks of Radius Book Group,
a Division of Diversion Publishing Corp.

CONTENTS

INTRODUCTION

This book is about winning elections. My goal is to describe the campaign strategies and tactics that are needed for a challenger to beat an incumbent. I wrote this book for candidates, political consultants, operatives, and campaigners who are out there around the world campaigning for change. Of course, incumbents themselves stand to benefit from this book, because it gives them the playbook of their opponents. The book is also of interest to any politico who wants to learn more about election campaigns, which I consider the heart and soul of a democracy.

Ever since I was a child, I felt strongly about election campaigns. When I was thirteen years old, I became active in the youth organization of a political party in Switzerland. This interest in politics led me to become a student of political science and brought me to Washington, DC. I have both studied and taught politics on three continents and in three languages. For the past seventeen years, I've been running my own political consulting business. In that capacity, I've helped candidates win dozens of competitive election and referendum campaigns in various countries (and I am not even counting one-off deals and the easy wins). My first client ran for city councillor and my latest, biggest accomplishment was winning a presidential election.

When I started to do this for a living, sometimes I couldn't sleep at night because I was so excited about my work. At 3:00 a.m., I would walk around in circles in my apartment with thoughts and ideas popping into my head one after the other. And today, after many years of doing this, I feel more passionate about campaigns than ever. Although I am a very political person, I try to keep my personal convictions private. I do so in my media interviews, on social media, in my publications, and in this book. That makes me a much more effective consultant. So, for instance, I refrain from mentioning my clients by name in this book, because I believe political consulting is a private and personal enterprise based on mutual trust. Despite keeping the names of my clients confidential, the case studies I present include accurate specifics such as the office in question, poll numbers, dialogues, as well as decisions and measures taken.

We can learn from election campaigns happening all over the world. When I was studying political science in Geneva, Switzerland in the 1990s, we had just started to use email and the Internet. At the time, comparative politics basically meant to compare France, Germany, and Italy. Only later when conducting initial research for my PhD dissertation did I discover an entire world of election campaigns. I distinctly remember the night when I was doing research at the George Washington University's Gelman Library in Washington, DC, and I did a search for the keywords "election campaign" and "Brazil." I was thunderstruck by how many articles popped up. It was like an intellectual awakening for me as I realized that something can be learned about election campaigns everywhere in the world.

US presidential elections are to politics what the Super Bowl or the World Cup are to sports: the most expensive, the most professional, and the hardest fought competition. Logically, therefore, US elections feature prominently in this book; but in addition, I also talk about examples and cases from Ukraine, the United Kingdom (UK), France, Germany, Spain and Brazil, to name a few, because they each offer unique insights.

While working on my PhD dissertation, I developed a model on how challengers can win elections against incumbents. In a nutshell, I compared successful challengers from the US, the Philippines, Brazil, and Germany with unsuccessful ones from the same countries. You may think that the contexts of political campaigns vary greatly from one country to another, and I agree that important differences with respect to the history, culture, and political system of a country do exist. My idea was to compare cases from countries that are as different as possible and look for patterns among both the winners and the losers. This is a so-called most different research design.

This book distills the model developed during my PhD research and enriches it with real-world campaign experience I've gained around the globe over the past two decades. I found that the successful candidates do indeed share striking similarities. They start to plan their campaigns earlier than the losing challengers, they are able to put the incumbents on the defensive, and they are successful in highlighting contrast and in formulating a message of change. They usually fight for and win ownership of the dominant issue, which is often the economy. I also discovered that the unsuccessful candidates, on the other hand, frequently commit the same mistakes. Some of them have not had much time to prepare for their campaigns because they have quickly risen to the national political scene. Others do not use the time at their disposal wisely, notably to neutralize the weaknesses of their respective candidacies. For various reasons, which I discuss later in detail, they are also hesitant or unable to contrast themselves with their respective incumbents, and they invest little time and effort into learning about modern campaigns or improving their skills on the campaign trail.

Can you learn how to play football from reading a book? No. Real learning takes a lot of application, practice, repetition, and therefore time. But if you read a book written by a football champion, it may inspire you, provide useful advice, and teach you pitfalls to look out for. Likewise, my own successes shed light on how to win a political campaign, and you will also learn a great deal from my losses—and there were indeed some painful ones.

The present book focuses on the strategic fundamentals of election campaigns, not on the latest buzz. Joseph Napolitan, a legendary American political consultant, used to say that there are three steps to winning any campaign: (1) decide what you are going to say, (2) decide how and to whom you are going to say it, and then (3) say it.[1] After long studies, a lot of research on the topic, many wins, and some losses, I am convinced that he was exactly right. I remember once conversing with a prospective client about this. "That is basic, Louis," said the congresswoman who was thinking about running for Senate. While that may be true, and while cliffhanger elections exist in which plenty of factors could theoretically have made the difference, most elections are won or lost on the basics. If you have a realistic chance of winning an election but end up losing, it's often because you did not effectively and correctly execute these steps or because you lost focus along the way. A lot of complexity is woven into the basics, and simple does not equal easy.

You might also wonder, "How about social media?" I hear it all the time and write about how to use it to your advantage, but the fact that technological changes are impacting campaigns is nothing new in itself. Radio changed the way campaigns were fought and won a hundred years ago. The same happened with the advent of television a few decades later. Technology will continue to evolve and probably at an increasingly fast pace. Artificial intelligence, for example, will impact the media and campaigns and thereby pose serious challenges. I'm of the opinion that candidates who are able to take full advantage of technological changes early on may be able to eke out a (tactical) win. While journalists and politicians alike are fond of these stories, it would be shortsighted to rely solely on technological know-how. It's wiser and more sustainable to learn the basics. As Jack Nicklaus—one of the best golfers in history—said: "Learn the fundamentals of the game and stick to them. Band-Aid remedies never last."[2] I agree 100 percent.

In this book, I use the terms "challenger" and "opposition candidate" synonymously. Depending on your country and political system, one may be more familiar to you than the other. You will read mostly about high-profile campaigns, including those of presidents, prime ministers, governors, senators, and congressmen. But many of the lessons learned also apply to local, down ballot campaigns with a smaller budget. In a local campaign, the tools available are different, but the fundamental dynamics are the same. You won't hear much about primary campaigns and intraparty competition, though many lessons apply equally there, and my governing perspective is that of a candidate and not a party. Some of the politicians taking center stage will be familiar to you, people about whom you may have a strong opinion, either positive or negative. Perhaps you may associate them with wrong decisions or even scandals. I encourage you to set these opinions aside as you read, in search of discoveries that can benefit you. This book is not about making a moral or political judgment; rather, together, we'll study these politicians as analytical political operatives. Like them or not, the politicians you read about in this book are some of the greatest campaigners and opposition candidates in history from around the world. Future candidates cannot and should not merely copy and paste the way these politicians ran their campaigns, but you can gain inspiration by looking at how they played—and won—the contest.

1

SHOULD I STAY OR SHOULD I GO?

If you bought this book, chances are that you are thinking about running for office. Should I run for reelection or try and run for higher office? Should I switch from the legislative to an executive position? Or, for newcomer candidates, should I leave a comfortable life as a private citizen and enter politics? These can be life-changing decisions, and I've spent countless hours with politicians discussing their next career moves. You may know the song "Should I Stay or Should I Go" by the Clash from the 1980s. Its lyrics are about love, but it perfectly expresses indecision and uncertainty, and many politicians could relate well. The purpose of this chapter is to bring some structure into the decision-making process about whether or not to run. If you are planning to go against an incumbent, a systematic analysis of the situation should start with an honest assessment of the incumbent's strengths and weaknesses. After that, I give you pointers on how to evaluate yourself as a possible challenger, followed by a framework to analyze the context and its dynamics.

HOW VULNERABLE IS THE INCUMBENT REALLY?

It's commonly said that elections with an incumbent are first of all a referendum on the incumbent. According to that approach, if voters are happy and satisfied with how things are currently going, the incumbent usually wins reelection. This is short of saying that in such a case, voters would barely even consider a challenger. "Never change a winning team" is a well-known proverb that expresses the point well. I have tested this myself many times in focus groups for incumbent mayors, governors, and presidents. If respondents describe the current situation in their country, province, or city using positive words, they often vote for the incumbent. In such a situation where the incumbent is really strong, it might be wise to wait for a better opportunity. If voters describe the current state of things more negatively, however, the vote is up for grabs for the challenger. Or put differently, dissatisfaction with the status quo is the raw material from which a challenger can build a successful argument for change.

Keep in mind that voters don't know what a challenger would really do if elected. It's been said that when voting for challengers, voters merely express a wish and hope that campaign promises will be fulfilled. When voters vote for an incumbent, on the other hand, they render a verdict on the performance they've observed during the past years. They can decide whether they want to renew the contract and keep the incumbent on the job or not. When Ronald Reagan ran to unseat incumbent president Jimmy Carter in 1980, he famously asked voters, "Are you better off than you were four years ago?" It makes sense to frame an election using a question like this, as it is meant to say that all voters who thought that they were not better off should vote for the challenger, Ronald Reagan. The statement illustrates this rationale of an incumbent election as a referendum very well, and after Reagan won a landslide victory, it became an inspiration for many challenger campaigns in the US and abroad.

Candidates are normally great at seeing their own strengths and their opponent's weaknesses, but objectivity about your own weaknesses and your opponent's strengths is just as essential. The first step is, therefore, to take an honest look at the incumbent and ask yourself if he can be beaten. You are probably thinking that everybody can be beaten, and while that is theoretically correct, the odds are against you. Incumbents enjoy several advantages over challengers and therefore often win reelection. During the past ten years, for example, more than 80 percent of incumbent US congressmen and senators beat their respective challengers.[3] In 2022, all incumbent US senators who ran for another term succeeded on election day. As for myself, I've only ever lost one incumbent campaign, for a state legislator in my early days as a consultant.

Let us therefore take a closer look at some aspects of the incumbency advantage that you should include in your assessment. To begin with, incumbents usually have high awareness and name recall. As a result, they are serious, viable candidates to their own succession. Holding an office has its own aura and series of advantages. Depending on the level of government, these advantages may be slight but even so are important and something a challenger doesn't have. In the case of presidents, they are usually called "Mister President" or "Madam President." They have bodyguards and drivers and travel with an entire caravan. This can indeed be hugely impressive. I distinctly remember when I consulted with a president for the first time. I arrived at the presidential palace, knowing that history had been made there. While waiting for the meeting together with another client of mine who had introduced me to the president, I looked at the paintings in the palace. When the president arrived for the meeting, everyone in the room stood up. You can't help but be starstruck.

Being an incumbent also usually makes fundraising a lot easier. I have never seen an incumbent who was not at least at eye level with the challenger in terms of campaign funds. More often, incumbents outspend challengers. This fundraising advantage is one of the main reasons why many local or congressional elections are not competitive. It's common for incumbents to use their big war chests to scare off would-be challengers from even entering the race. In many instances, those seats only become competitive again once the incumbent ceases to run for reelection.

Being an incumbent also opens up opportunities for strategic agenda setting. One can tactically plan important meetings, summits, or events in order to get (positive) media coverage. Incumbents also have staff, advisers, an organization, and experiences from previous campaigns. In some countries, the incumbent controls redistricting or even the electoral calendar. Under the British model, for example, the incumbent can more or less freely decide during the term when to hold the elections. Obviously, they will call for the election when the political climate is favorable for their party. I've worked for an opposition candidate in an Asian country following that model, and it's a considerable disadvantage. We would hear rumors that the election might take place soon, and prepare accordingly, only to find out that there would be no election. If the elections are finally being called, they will then normally take place within weeks in that system, leaving little time to mount a powerful campaign.

Incumbent governments in less-developed democracies sometimes even use parts of the government apparatus to their advantage. In places where voters must register to vote, control over that process can be (ab)used. Government employees or recipients of government projects are sometimes pressured to vote for the incumbent. The police also occasionally play a role—for example, to harass the opposition and to intimidate voters. Opposition candidates may suddenly find it difficult to find venues to hold meetings or means of transportation. I've had clients forced to deal with that. It is a topic for another book.

All that said, incumbents also face some distinct disadvantages. Let us now take a closer look at those. Incumbents are usually

STRENGTHS AND WEAKNESSES OF AN INCUMBENT

• In some countries has the ability to control the electoral calendar	• Is held responsible by voters for the status quo, in particular a bad economy
• Has universal name recall, awareness	• Has a government record to defend
• Is ex officio a legitimate candidate	• Might have enacted unpopular policies
• Can use the aura of the office	• Has to justify broken campaign promises from last election
• Has significant fundraising opportunities	• Risks appearing out of touch
• Has unique ability to get media attention	• Is caught in scandals or faces allegations (for example, corruption, misconduct, illegal fundraising, abuse of power)
• Has staff to run daily operations	• Has to deal with wear and tear in office
	• Party base risks being demoralized (losses in local, midterm, or by-elections)

automatically associated with the status quo. When things are going well, and there is peace, safety, and a booming economy, this is wind at the back of an incumbent and his approval ratings. When things do not go well, the incumbent government often gets blamed for it, whether or not it's fair. While political decisions do have an impact on the economy, so do plenty of other factors that a president or prime minister, let alone a governor or mayor, cannot influence. After the financial crisis of 2008, for example, it was a difficult environment for many incumbents, almost independently from their political ideology and from how they dealt with the crisis. During the years following the crisis, incumbents lost, sometimes brutally, in Greece, Hungary, the UK, Ireland, Portugal, Spain, and France. Many of them lost their reelection bids in part because voters were unhappy with how things were going. I also think, and I write about this later in the book, that COVID-19, by and large, cost Donald Trump reelection to the White House. In such a situation of an economic, health, or international crisis, it is crucial for incumbents to show that they at least understand what voters are thinking and might be going through. Depending on the situation, a way out might be to try and shift blame onto someone else or to scare voters into thinking that no matter how bad things are, everything might get even worse with a new government. While some strategic options are available, which I discuss later in the book, it is a tough spot to be in for an incumbent when voters are unhappy with the status quo.

In addition to challenging circumstances and crises, incumbents face even more specific disadvantages. An incumbent has, by definition, a record of decisions and actions to defend, some of which might be unpopular with key voters. In my industry, we call this a policy disagreement. An example of this is Barack Obama's health-care reform, which became known as Obamacare. After getting elected, Obama was able to push the corresponding legislation through both chambers of Congress and it became the law of the land. Among voters, though, the law was polarizing and one of the reasons why Democrats lost the succeeding midterm elections. Other decisions may be popular at the beginning and only grow to become polarizing over time. An example of this is the case of George W. Bush and the war in Iraq. Following the 9/11 terrorist attacks on the US, the general sentiment of public opinion supported military action in Iraq and the removal from office of Saddam Hussein. This substantially changed over time as the operation seemed to drag on and American casualties rose.[4] By the time American voters went to the polls for the midterm elections, the war had become a heavy burden hanging around the neck of President Bush and Republican candidates. As a result, Democrats won control in both the House of Representatives and the Senate. Once the incumbent party loses in the midterms, it weakens the authority of the incumbent within his party. In other political systems, a similar effect results when the incumbent party loses important local elections. Party members get nervous, and talk of a challenge to the leadership begins to rise.

An incumbent might also be challenged specifically with respect to promises made during the previous campaign. Some promises may have been kept while others have been broken as circumstances changed. A part of the incumbent's base might be disappointed that the leader could not keep all promises and instead had to compromise along the way. When Petro Poroshenko first ran for president of Ukraine in 2014, he promised that he could end the war in Eastern Ukraine within a few months. By the time he ran for reelection in 2019, the war was still ongoing, and voters were incredibly angry about the broken promise. This contributed to a humiliating loss for the incumbent to a political newcomer and comedian, Volodymyr Zelensky.

Incumbents also run the risk of appearing arrogant or out of touch with regular voters. French voters, for example, were staggered when they learned that the personal hairdresser of their president, François Hollande, earned a salary of close to 10,000 euro per month, which was similar to the paycheck of a government minister.[5] Incumbents also have to deal with scandals. Frequent allegations include misconduct in office, illegal fundraising, secret bank accounts, or abuse of government money for private purposes. For US presidents, such scandals can culminate in an impeachment, as was the case with Donald Trump (Ukraine quid pro quo and the January 6 attacks on the Capitol), Bill Clinton (Monica Lewinsky sex scandal), and Richard Nixon (Watergate break-in). The increase of video recording capacities has only made allegations more common. Former Finnish prime minister Sanna Marin faced accusations and had to take a drug test after footage of her boisterously dancing at a private party became public. Pictures showing Boris Johnson at lockdown parties were at least part of the reason for his ousting as prime minister of the UK. In Austria, a secretly recorded video ended the first government of Chancellor Sebastian Kurz and personal WhatsApp chats becoming public his second.

CAN YOU BEAT THE INCUMBENT?

Next, let us turn our attention to the situation of a challenger. Not every challenger is equal; there are important differences, most notably with respect to awareness, funding, and experience. I would therefore like to introduce to you the concept of *challenger quality*. Good challengers make up for at least some of the incumbent advantages. Celebrities running for office, for example, bring the advantage to the table that they already have high awareness, even if it does not equate automatically to a presumption of political competence. I've worked for famous athletes, actors, and beauty queens turned politicians and can confirm from my own experience that high awareness is nevertheless an advantage, which a noncelebrity candidate has to first build up. A good example of this is Ukrainian president Volodymyr Zelensky. Before entering politics, Zelensky was a famous comedian and TV star. The presidency was the first office he had ever run for, but by the time he officially announced his candidacy, he had long been a household name. As in the case of Zelensky, celebrity candidates have a unique capability to get media attention. The mere fact that they consider running for office can generate media coverage that a traditional politician can only dream of. Journalists will gladly cover celebrities since fame is one of the main drivers of today's media, which is constantly looking for clicks. Another good example is Donald Trump. When he first announced his candidacy for the Republican nomination for president, he was a well-known businessman and media personality. Due to his fame and provocative statements, his sixteen primary opponents soon struggled to get any media attention at all.

The next crucial consideration is funding: quality challengers occasionally self-fund their own campaigns. Thaksin Shinawatra was one of the richest men in Thailand before he entered politics, founded a new party, and became prime minister. Years earlier, Silvio Berlusconi in Italy had pursued the same route—he was a successful businessman who entered politics, founded a new party, and became prime minister. Now, being rich and self-funding a campaign does not guarantee victory. In the last US presidential election, two candidates competing in the Democratic primaries were extremely wealthy individuals. Michael Bloomberg and Tom Steyer could, by and large, write a check for themselves for any amount, yet neither one came near winning the nomination. Self-funding a campaign nonetheless gives important freedom. Even if poll numbers are not great, a self-funded campaign is not at risk of running out of money and can continue. Voters also generally associate self-funding a campaign with the liberty of the candidates to speak their own mind. A candidate that is not able (or willing) to self-fund can make up for it with fundraising capability. I talk more about money in politics in chapter 6, but for now, you should be aware that most candidates dislike this aspect of campaigning and that it takes a serious commitment, discipline, and lots of time.

While the capability to raise funds definitely helps a challenger, money cannot buy political experience, including the experience of previously having run for office. Candidates who have already run and won an election enjoy the benefit of having a campaign team, or at least elements of one. High-quality challengers therefore often have some political experience, perhaps at the state or local level. They have been governor of a state or may have served in parliament. Newcomers to politics often think wrongly that anyone who has common sense can run for office. Well, while political marketing is not an exact science, knowledge and experience do come into play.

It's also crucial not to underestimate the brutality of a high-profile race and the ruthlessness of the media that comes with it. Previous and local campaign experience can give candidates an inkling of the issues that will be raised against them and of what they should prepare for. My assessment is therefore clear: the best challengers run for local or statewide office, win reelection overwhelmingly, and then try to climb the ladder. Winning reelection decisively is important because it sends a clear signal of readiness and broad appeal.

Some candidates lose reelection or avoid running for it out of fear of losing but then nevertheless try to run for higher office. This is almost always a losing game plan. Mitt Romney, for example, served as governor of Massachusetts. While he was popular at the beginning, his job approval percentage sank to the mid-30s toward the end of his term.[6] He decided not to run for reelection as governor but to seek the Republican nomination for president instead. Despite spending more than $100 million during his primary campaign, which at the time represented a big war chest, Romney lost the nomination to John McCain.

DO YOU REALLY WANT TO DO THIS TO YOURSELF?

Let me also challenge you as to why you want to run for office. People say that three fundamental things drive candidates: power, ego, and money. In my observation, this is absolutely right, and it is often a combination of the three. Please do not get me wrong—I don't mean this in a cynical way. There is nothing wrong with this per se, since, after all, we are all human. It is important, though, to be honest with yourself. In addition to the motives I just mentioned, there is a series of more pragmatic reasons why candidates run for office:

- to mobilize a certain group of voters (for example, a candidate who wants to engage Hispanic voters in the political process)
- to prepare for a future campaign (for example, a candidate knows that it will be difficult to win but runs nevertheless to become known and lay the groundwork for a next, more promising candidacy)
- to promote an issue (for example, a candidate who feels strongly about immigration or gender equality)
- to help your party (this is often the case in a country where voters vote for a party list and the party needs additional candidates to fill up their lists)
- to protect business interests
- to get publicity (there was a time when porn stars ran for office in Italy under the banner of the Love Party. Other European countries had the Anti-PowerPoint Party, the German Beer Drinkers Union, and the Party of the Nonvoters)
- because of a lack of other options (this happens in countries with term limits; a candidate will run for another office because of term limits for the office currently held)
- simply wanting to be in the game (for example, a young politician who planned to run for office sometime and wants to get started, or a candidate who regrets not having run before)
- to protect a stronghold (for example, the mayoralty of a town)
- to prevent the opponent from winning
- to hold your place within the party (a candidate knows that winning will be unlikely but runs nevertheless to remain as leader of the party)

I also think that goals should be ambitious but realistic. For example, I've worked for a party in an Asian country that has been the opposition for decades, and its leaders have made themselves comfortable in the isolation and powerlessness of the opposition. They were excited about giving a speech and argued passionately about who would run in what district, but everyone knew deep down that they would lose. This feels wrong to me. Tony Blair, former prime minister of the UK, correctly says that while it can be exciting to dominate the media agenda while in opposition, you ultimately need to win elections and be in power if you are serious about realizing your plans. Or, as he puts it, "In opposition, you wake up and ask, 'What shall I say today?' In government, you ask 'What shall I do today?'"[7]

This said, many politicians do enjoy the election campaign a lot. It must feel electric when hundreds of thousands of people applaud and cheer after your speech, as happened to a client of mine who successfully ran for president. Even in a campaign that is less high profile, being invited as a guest of honor can be pleasant, or an ad or photo shoot can be fun. Be that as it may, I also want to be straightforward in saying that running for office has another side to it, which is brutal. If you are serious about running, you will be spending much more time with your campaign staff than with your spouse and children for months to come. You will be constantly tired, and you will spend a great amount of your time asking other people for money like a beggar.

Once you run for office, everyone around you—in particular, your donors—will feel free to give you unsolicited advice on how your ad should look, what you should wear, or how you can become a better speaker. I remember a very wealthy client of mine complaining about that: "Why do I have to listen to all these idiots telling me what to do when I am ten times richer than they are?" he asked, exhausted on a late-evening call. Depending on how high profile the race is, you will face scrutiny by the media. People will investigate and report and comment on your private life, your looks, your weight, your clothing, and things that happened thirty years ago in your life. Get ready to see stories appear in the media about your sex life, about your children, and about business matters no one would otherwise care about.

As a result, I have asked many potential candidates—do you really want to do this to yourself?

Do not fall into the trap of thinking that all you have to do is to survive the campaign for a few months and all this will be over. In the event that you're successful, this is the moment when the scrutiny will start for good and everything you say and do will be challenged and criticized. It is also likely that, sooner or later after you start serving, wild speculations about your health or other matters will be spread around and whispered about. Many clients also tell me after winning and once they start to serve that they have never worked harder in their lives. If you run for parliament, you might win but find yourself in the minority, and as a result, you will have limited power and impact in your country's capital. On a personal note, I suggest that if you have skeletons in the closet, you should already be thinking about a communications plan on how to deal with them. Chances are, it will become public, and it's always better to be in the driver's seat and tell the story yourself.

It's sometimes amazing how naive newcomers to electoral politics are. Almost every week, I get emails from people who are new to politics and want to run. They talk about honorable intentions to serve, about great plans and proposals, and about how they want to save their state and constituents. Well, it is certainly good to have ideas and plans, and it is even better if you have something distinct to offer your voters. The reality of electoral politics is different, however. I have seen people's lives literally ripped apart after they entered public life or tried to run for higher office, and in that respect, social media has not made things better. Few people have to accept more insults than politicians. It has become widespread and commonly tolerated to bash and trash politicians online. If you are serious about running for office, you will need a very thick skin.

I often ask candidates how much they want to win, ranking themselves on a scale from one to ten, and surprisingly, not all say ten. Some instantly say twelve, but others pause for a moment and then say seven or eight. Without any doubt, they would all take a win, so let me reformulate: is your desire to win so great that you will do whatever it takes, including things you dislike? This may include going through a dry run for a debate for the seventh time, spending hours asking people for money, or facing a hostile interviewer.

Alastair Campbell, a former communications adviser to Tony Blair, points out that sports and electoral politics have an important thing in common: it's win or lose, there's no middle ground, and therefore it's all about winning. He carried out an interesting study comparing winners from politics, sports, and the private economic sector. He found that one trait shared by many winners is that they really hate losing. As a matter of fact, they are as scared as hell to lose.[8]

The mirror opposite of what Campbell describes would be candidates who are overconfident. Some candidates look at elections as God's verdict. More often than not, they lose. In that sense, I would rather work for a candidate or party that is slightly behind but on top of things and working hard than for a candidate or party that is ahead but complacent. As a consultant, this desire to win is also something that is difficult to change. Candidates can be arrogant, thrifty, or chaotic. I have learned over the years how to deal with it, but they "gotta wanna" as is said in the US to express passion and perseverance.

ASSESSING THE CONTEXT AND ITS DYNAMICS

Election campaigns are not isolated events but take place in a wider political, economic, and societal context. In that respect, I would like to introduce you to Theda Skocpol, a social scientist at Harvard University, who did significant research on social revolutions. Her approach is quite different from how history has usually been taught in schools with a focus on dates, events, and the key players. In a nutshell, she says that revolutions are not made—they happen. She pays particular attention to the structural conditions that exist within a country prior to a revolution. If certain conditions are present, revolutions unfold.[9] I am talking about this because I see a similarity with election campaigns in which a challenger goes against an incumbent. Do candidates, smart consultants, and campaign teams really make electoral victories? Or do victories happen because of circumstances?

In the past, political scientists would have answered that campaigners have little influence on the outcome of an election. The dominant paradigm among academics in the US and elsewhere was to prove that election campaigns do not matter. Their argument was that key factors such as the state of the economy, the state of international affairs (war or peace), the price of oil, and the duration of the incumbency could be used to predict the outcome of the election. Think about it: if it is possible to accurately forecast the outcome of the election months prior to election day, before the actual campaign takes place, then the campaign can hardly have had much of an impact. It sounds logical, and for quite some time such predictions were pretty accurate.

Professor Allan J. Lichtman is a historian and political scientist at American University in Washington, DC. In his groundbreaking book *Predicting the Next President: The Keys to the White House*, he argues that the outcome of a presidential election depends almost entirely on the performance of the incumbent government party.[10] In other words, Professor Lichtman says that governing is much more important than campaigning. As the title of his book indicates, he developed thirteen "keys" to the White House. When five or fewer of these statements are false, the incumbent governing party is predicted to win the popular vote of the presidential election. On the other hand, when six or more are false, the opposition party is predicted to win the popular vote. Professor Lichtman has accurately predicted every presidential election from 1984 until 2020. While the model is obviously made for the specific case of US presidential elections, I think that it is worthwhile to look at his keys in some detail and consider how this applies to your case:

- Incumbent-party mandate: After the midterm elections, the incumbent party holds more seats in the House of Representatives than it did after the previous midterm elections.
- Nomination contest: There is no serious contest for the incumbent-party nomination.
- Incumbency: The incumbent-party candidate is the sitting president.
- Third party: There is no significant third-party or independent campaign.
- Short-term economy: The economy is not in recession during the election campaign.
- Long-term economy: Real annual per capita economic growth during the term equals or exceeds mean growth during the two previous terms.
- Policy change: The incumbent administration effects major changes in national policy.
- Social unrest: There is no sustained social unrest during the term.
- Scandal: The incumbent administration is untainted by major scandal.
- Foreign or military failure: The incumbent administration suffers no major failure in foreign or military affairs.
- Foreign or military success: The incumbent administration achieves a major success in foreign or military affairs.
- Incumbent charisma: The incumbent-party candidate is charismatic or a national hero.

- Challenger charisma: The challenging-party candidate is not charismatic or a national hero.[11]

I personally argue that several of these aspects are impacted by campaigning, at least partially; what voters perceive and remember as a major scandal might depend on effective crisis management. Whether a candidate is seen as charismatic is not set in stone but can be influenced. A lack of charisma can be dealt with and neutralized by the candidate, a point which I discuss in chapter 6. Even how voters perceive the state of the economy is something that can be shaped by the campaign team. While official figures exist, the news and communication about them are subject to more or less effective spin-doctoring. This is also particularly true with respect to the blame game, meaning the question of whom voters hold responsible for a lack of economic performance. Barack Obama's reelection campaign comes to mind. The state of the economy was rather mediocre by the time he ran for reelection, but he was effective at blaming his predecessor and the conditions he inherited for it. Whether or not there is significant intraparty or third-party competition might also be the result of effective campaigning. I am willing to concede that a good campaign may not necessarily make you win, but a bad campaign can definitely make you lose and they therefore must matter to a certain extent.

With respect to forecast models, I also notice that in the US and in many other countries, extremely close and upset elections have become more frequent. In Germany, for example, few observers would have predicted even a few months before the 2021 federal election that a Social Democrat would be the next chancellor. In the 2017 French legislative elections, the established parties basically collapsed, and a new one appeared out of nowhere and took power. Such triumphs are furthered by important societal changes that are taking place. Public opinion in many countries is becoming increasingly volatile, and identification with parties is decreasing. The way voters consume and absorb news is changing as well. Nowadays, there is no longer one dominant national TV channel with broadly watched evening news. Voters have a plethora of channels and media outlets to choose from, national and international, online or offline, nonstop around the clock. For some time, we were in a so-called pick-and-choose culture, where voters chose the news items they found appealing. Now we live in an era when, due to algorithms, voters are increasingly only being served the news bites that they like. All this makes campaigning more worthwhile, maybe more exciting, but also more demanding than ever.

HOW TO READ A SURVEY TO MAKE AN ULTIMATE DECISION

After you have conducted a comprehensive assessment of the incumbent, your quality as a challenger, and the context, it's time to conduct a survey in order to make an ultimate decision. In the US, polls have been notoriously wrong for several election cycles. While the same has happened in other countries as well, this does not mean that the laws of statistics would no longer apply. In that sense, it makes me chuckle when people say that they "believe" or "don't believe" in surveys. I sometimes ask back if they believe in physics or chemistry. Rather than a matter of conviction, the key is to know what a survey legitimately can and cannot tell us and how to distinguish methodologically solid ones from sloppy ones. Politicians often have a love-hate relationship with surveys, mostly depending on whether results are encouraging for them. If results are positive, they sometimes ignore all limitations of market research. If results are negative, on the other hand, they dismiss the research in question altogether. Let us therefore clear up some of the basics.

The bigger the sample size, the smaller the margin of error. My rule of thumb is that six hundred respondents is the minimum for a survey in a locality. I have never conducted a stand-alone survey with a sample size smaller than that. Let us assume that you have a survey with a randomized sample of six hundred respondents, a margin of error of ± 4 percent, and your candidate gets 42 percent of the vote. This means that the vote share of that candidate among the entire population is between 38 percent (42 – 4) and 46 percent (42 + 4). In fact, since a confidence level of 95 percent has become industry standard, it means that with a probability of 95 percent, the vote is within the range of 38 percent and 46 percent, and there is a 5 percent chance that results are outside of that range. Nothing more and nothing less. There are politicians who don't care about the margin of error and run surveys with incredibly small sample sizes. The margin of error then becomes so big that the data may look scientific but is practically meaningless. On the other hand, some candidates are fond of huge sample sizes. For presidential candidates, for example, I've conducted surveys with several thousand respondents. This is far from wrong, but it becomes expensive.

The next aspect to consider is how the fieldwork is being conducted. Traditionally, data was gathered through telephone interviews. This has become increasingly difficult with more and more people screening calls and only having mobile phones. While online polls have gained popularity, I am skeptical because of the bias against segments of the electorate that are less frequently online. I have worked in several developing countries, and my survey interviews there are conducted in person. It's the slowest way to gather data but by far the most reliable one.

Another issue that is linked to data gathering is the weighing of raw data. In recent US elections, this was often the root of the problem: assumptions about participation levels of certain segments of the electorate turned out to be wrong. Every new election cycle, pollsters claim to have learned their lesson and to now apply supposedly more accurate weighing, when it's obvious that this does not solve the problem. In the countries where I work, I rarely weigh raw data when I conduct a poll. I rather invest a lot of attention into building solid fieldwork partnerships to make sure the randomization is guaranteed and the sampling and data collection are done properly.

It is important to get all these things right, so do not even consider doing the survey by yourself or by using students or employees. It's one of the top mistakes among new candidates. Conducting a survey is a science, and you therefore have two options: either you are running a high-profile campaign and you can afford to purchase a professional survey company, or you are an ad hoc campaign and you must rely on your gut feeling. To make strategic decisions based on wrong numbers however is entirely misguided.

A great deal of the success I'm able to bring to campaigns is also due to my unique use of qualitative opinion research, so-called focus group discussions. While a survey tells you *how many* voters think what, focus groups tell you the *why* behind the numbers. A focus group usually consists of about eight respondents. They are not a bunch of friends gathered together but a carefully defined and recruited target group. We usually conduct a series of focus groups and look for patterns, which almost always become apparent. Based on their data, I have told clients what projects to focus on, how to name them, how to make up for mistakes during a crisis, and how to take advantage of the competition's weaknesses. Focus groups have revealed to me what campaign tools to use, what ads to air, and how to tweak them to make them more effective. I have even used them to explore how to change the physical appearance or behavior of the top candidate.

That said, every serious election campaign should start with a feasibility study and baseline research. In reality, candidates are often hesitant to conduct a poll because, one, it costs money, and two, they are afraid to see the results. Regarding the costs, this is a good test; if you are serious about running and it's more than a dream, by all means you will have to either raise money or spend your own. As for the fear of seeing the true survey numbers, I always tell candidates that reality is the best starting point to plan a campaign. It happens often that candidates want to "go around" first and "test the waters." They want to spread campaign literature or even run ads before taking a baseline survey. A client of mine once said that this approach comes with a price tag. He is absolutely right, and this price tag has three dimensions: money, time (that you can't recover), and opportunity cost.

A candidate who wants to start campaigning without baseline research is like a pilot who says, "I do not need the navigation system to take off. I will turn it on once I am up in the sky and no longer know where I am." Good luck with that! Moreover, if you do not know where you are starting, how do you know that you are making progress? Or making enough progress in view of your efforts and spending? In other words, these candidates often misunderstand the purpose of a survey. They think that the survey is there to "prove" to themselves and their allies that they are winning when it's rather a basis for their decision-making and planning.

The reason to do a baseline survey in this sense is to find out where you really stand. Telling candidates their true awareness level, favorability rating, and vote share is often a key contribution I make because most new candidates overestimate their own support. In addition, one gets other important benefits from a baseline survey. It can indicate your perceived strengths and weaknesses as well as those of your opponents. It can also test different possible scenarios, show opinions of voters on main issues, measure the power of possible endorsements, and tell you how many and what kind of voters are up for grabs.

The overall campaign budget determines how often you should conduct research and with what design. If you run a small campaign and you have an overall budget of US$100,000, then it barely makes sense to spend half of it on public opinion research. On the other hand, if you have a war chest of US$10 million, it's foolish not to conduct a series of surveys as a basis for making informed decisions on how to spend those funds. As a rule of thumb, it makes sense to allocate 10–15 percent of the overall campaign budget to public opinion research. In a presidential campaign, 10–15 percent of the campaign budget can mean regular tracking and in-depth local polling. In a local campaign, if resources are scarce, this can reasonably mean a baseline and one tracking survey.

When analyzing results, it is also important to put them into the right context. Surveys are a snapshot and never a prediction of the result. This is particularly important for a race where a challenger goes against an incumbent because there is often an imbalance between the candidates with respect to recognition. Surveys that are taken months before an election mostly reflect the levels of voter awareness of the candidates. Since incumbents are usually more known than challengers, they are often ahead in the vote question. This is why, when I look at a survey, I do not care as much about where my client stands at the moment as I do about their potential to grow their vote share.

In order to measure the strength of the incumbency as we discussed earlier in this chapter, it is useful to assess the incumbents on their own and irrespective of the challengers. A standard question to do that concerns job approval: "Do you rather approve or disapprove of the job Governor X is doing?" In my experience, incumbents often end up with a vote share on election day that is close to their job approval. I have worked in countries where voters are exceedingly generous in giving high approval ratings. As a result, I had clients with literally 90 percent job approval (yes, in democracies). In the US and in many other countries, voters are much more cynical. There, the benchmark for incumbents is 50 percent. If they can garner a majority of voters approving of the job they are doing, they are in good shape heading into reelection. If an incumbent's job approval rating drops below 50 percent, on the other hand, this is considered dangerous territory.

It's our professional obligation to be honest with clients and tell them if the data shows that their chances of winning are small. This doesn't mean that they should run away from a challenge. Some candidates start out far behind and end up winning. In my practice, I've directly told a few people that they should not run and counter-intuitively, they became my biggest fans. The reason for that is that potential candidates rarely hear someone telling them not to run. Most people will encourage you to run, tell you that you can win, and promise you their vote. They do that because they think it's what you want to hear, because they benefit from your running, and because they have zero downside in doing so. The risk of losing is solely with the candidate. All those voices should therefore be taken not with a grain of salt, but with lots of salt. A client of mine correctly says this: "In politics, the only one who cares about you is yourself." I'm afraid he has a point. So, when I told these few individuals that they should not run, it was something they felt deep inside, but no one else had told them. It saved them a lot of time, money, and humiliation. They were forever grateful.

LAST PIECE OF ADVICE

If you decide that it's not the right time for you to run, then stick to your decision. Close this book and enjoy the saved money, the spared hassle, and the extra time with friends and family. What you shouldn't do is change your mind and enter the race at the last moment. I have seen it happen several times: potential candidates are hesitant to run, do not carry out the necessary groundwork, and tell everyone (including themselves) that they will not run. Then, at the last minute, they cannot resist the temptation and jump into the race. Oftentimes, they end up losing brutally. I do not want you to be like them.

2

PUTTING TOGETHER A WINNING CHALLENGER MESSAGE AND STRATEGY

Putting together a campaign can be both exciting and overwhelming. I have advised and coached more than a hundred politicians and candidates. Clients include presidents, vice presidents, a Miss Universe winner and a runner-up, actors, celebrities, businessmen, and some of the world's best-paid athletes. With all those experiences behind me, I've come to find an important constant, namely that most successful challenger campaigns have a crystal-clear message and a coherent strategy for delivering it to a specific target. What sounds simple on paper, however, is not often easy to carry out in reality. In this chapter, I discuss how to go about it, how to define your target audience, and how to develop your campaign message.

WHEN SHOULD I START?

When candidates ask me about the right moment to start campaigning, my answer is always the same: in seventeen years as a political consultant, I've never seen a candidate lose an election because they started planning too early. Opposition candidates in particular benefit from long campaigns (or extensive pre-campaigns if the official campaign period is limited by law) as they are often less known than incumbents. While some candidates are eager to run and cannot wait to do something, others are more hesitant. Over the years, I've witnessed several reasons why candidates wait to start preparations and planning. The most obvious one is because of funds. Planning a campaign means hiring staff and consultants in order to assemble a team, putting up a state-of-the-art website, and taking a survey. It also includes producing campaign materials and traveling to hold events. All this has a price tag, and some candidates either do not want to spend their own money or are unwilling to start raising funds. Others delay strategic planning because they are caught up in their daily business, and still others think that the impact of early campaign activities will be forgotten by election day. In some countries, candidates worry about peaking too early in the surveys. This strikes me as ridiculous. There is no such thing as peaking too early, but there can be a wrong interpretation of an early lead in the surveys. As the discussion of polling in the last chapter revealed, this lead might reflect an advantage in awareness but not in solid support.

An early onset is, of course, no guarantee of victory. Some candidates start early but do the wrong things and then end up losing. For example, I think that elaborate policy papers are nice to have and might help in governing or legislating once elected, but they do not prepare a candidate for a competitive election campaign. Voters want to get a sense of where a candidate stands, but few will ever read detailed papers. Having them can even make you vulnerable to possible attacks.

There might also be good reasons to wait to make the official announcement of your candidacy. Some candidates do not want to declare officially because they want to avoid becoming a target too early. Fair enough. You might also decide to hold off with your official announcement if you are the presumptive front-runner and such a strategy allows you to freeze the field of possible other candidates. The goal of that tactic is to leave your potential competitors in the dark about your real plans until it is too late for them to put together an effective campaign (while maintaining all your options). These might all be smart tactics, but it does not mean that holding off to make an official announcement should keep you from planning strategically. The empirical evidence is overwhelmingly clear that political marketing works best with a long-term perspective. I usually tell clients, "If you are not the front-runner now, what keeps you from making yourself the front-runner?"

I emphasize the case for early planning for a specific reason: election campaigns are extremely chaotic operations. If the race is competitive, and once it starts in earnest, it will feel like a roller-coaster ride, and a clear plan and strategy will help tremendously in managing the chaos. If you don't have a plan once the race begins, you will not be able to execute one later. Chances are that in such a case, your campaign will be put on the defense, and you will be caught in a modus operandi where you are mostly reacting to events. Also, while many politicians think that money is the most important resource in a campaign, I've come to realize that time is even more important. You can always raise more money, but you can never get back lost time. I have turned down substantial business from clients who have approached me when it was too late, a couple of weeks before the election. I knew that time had run out and that they would end up losing. Starting an operation has no point for me when the patient is already dead.

WHAT REALLY IS AN ELECTION CAMPAIGN?

When candidates and their teams start putting together a campaign, they often think about it in terms of producing advertising materials or trying to get media coverage. In many cases, one of the first questions candidates ask me is what their slogan should be. Others have heard—and believe—that social media can supposedly create miracles, so they hire a digital advertising agency. Yes, ads, social media, public relations (PR), and slogans are all part of an election campaign, but what, really, is an election campaign? Twenty years ago, my professor at the Graduate School of Political Management in Washington, DC, Dr. Ronald Faucheux, taught me a simple, yet convincing definition: an election campaign is a series of strategic decisions. A campaign should therefore be understood, thought of, and planned in terms of a series of strategic decisions. What decisions are we talking about? I mean the decisions regarding your goal, target audience, message, and plan you carry out in order to communicate your message to your audience.

Almost all campaign teams think they understand this and have a strategy, but many do not. They may have a schedule, a budget, and an action plan, but not in the sense of Faucheux's strategic decisions. In campaign-planning sessions, numerous hours are spent discussing details that don't matter. Should the candidate wear a different tie or no tie at all? What giveaway should the campaign produce? Literally everyone who has been involved in an actual campaign can think of examples like this, where conversations about small details turned around in circles forever. Yet I cannot think of any candidate who has lost an election because of the tie or because of the giveaway the campaign produced. James Carville and Paul Begala, two US consultants who were credited with Bill Clinton's win in 1992, say that the main problem in a campaign is that "the people you're trying to reach don't understand what you're trying to say."[12] I agree and would like to add that variations of this basic challenge include when the target audience forgets what you are trying to say or does not want to hear it, or if your message doesn't connect with them on an emotional level.

Only a handful of people usually really matter with respect to strategy development. I call this small group that makes the fundamental decisions *the strategic brain* of the campaign. I have worked for a successful presidential candidate with plenty of staff and enormous budgets, but for the longest time, there were barely more than a handful of people in my presentations. It sometimes takes me a while to figure out who really belongs to the strategic brain or who *should* belong to it. The spouse of the candidate, for example, may not appear in the organizational chart of the campaign but de facto is often part of the strategic brain.

It is also important that the people who form the strategic brain realize that, together, they are the strategic brain of the campaign. They must go through the process of reaching strategic decisions and developing a message together. Everyone ultimately has to be on the same page. Personal agenda, turf wars, or competition over funds unfortunately often gets in the way of real strategy planning. If no real debate takes place in strategy meetings, it's also a warning sign. Members of the team may end up sabotaging decisions later on at the implementation level. I have also experienced painful campaigns in which the message was decided by compromise among a whole bunch of (competing) consultants. If you want a sure way to lose an election, that's it. A message and a strategy should be coherent, edgy, and cohesive. They cannot be done by compromise. They are also not something that a low-level staffer can write for the top candidate and his team. They have to grow organically out of an intense process in which the key people are involved. Once this is done, it is nevertheless crucial that both the campaign message and strategy are written down. In that respect, I remember Faucheux's simple rule: if the campaign message and strategy are not written down in a campaign plan and agreed on, a campaign does not have a strategy. It will melt away rapidly during the heat and chaos of the campaign.

HOW MANY VOTES DOES IT TAKE YOU TO WIN?

If you are planning your campaign systematically, the first step is to determine how many votes it would take for you to win. Sound obvious? In my experience, at least half of the candidates do not know how many votes it takes for them to win the election. This is always bewildering to me because I think that it's impossible to plan an effective campaign if you don't know the target you are trying to reach.

It is of course impossible to know in advance exactly how many votes it will take to win. This depends on the turnout, the competitiveness of the races, your opponent(s), and other issues on the ballot on the same day. You should nevertheless make an assumption based on past results. For that, I suggest you look at the last three election cycles at a minimum and check how many votes the winner attained for the office you're eyeing. When you do this, you also have to consider the dynamics of the electoral system. In a country like the US with the so-called first-past-the-post system in which the candidate with the plurality of votes wins, this is straightforward. Other electoral systems are more complicated, with voters voting for party lists. In Switzerland, for example, we have the so-called open list system when voting for parliament. Voters can give two votes to the same candidate, delete candidates, or make their own list with a mix of candidates from different parties. This complicates matters and has to be considered when making a calculation. In some countries, voters can put candidates in order of priority, which again changes the equation. Much of this will be an educated guess, but *you need to figure out a specific, concrete number representing votes it will likely take for you to win.* This number has to be written down in your campaign plan.

Once you have a specific number of needed votes, you have to specify the coalition of target voters that you have to win over in order to reach that number of votes. The baseline survey I mentioned in the previous chapter plays an important role here because it will tell you the vote share and therefore the number of votes you would get if the election were held today. Ideally, the baseline survey will also tell you how many of those votes are solidly yours and how many are soft, meaning how many voters say they could still change their mind. It should further inform you about the vote share of your competitor(s) and about how many voters are completely undecided at that point in time. Many countries, including the US, have become increasingly polarized in recent years. As a result, fewer voters are truly undecided. The baseline survey should also tell you the sociodemographic profile of each of these voter categories and will therefore serve as a basis for your targeting strategy. This is often a difficult decision for campaign teams. They want to talk to all voters, but in most cases, this is unrealistic. Candidates often underestimate the amount of effort it takes to be heard by voters, meaning the time and repetition it takes until a message registers with the electorate. You probably do not have the money or the time to do that, nor do all voters want to hear from you. It is therefore usually more effective to communicate repeatedly with a limited number of voters than to talk less often with all the voters. "Beat the big story hard" is a common motto among journalists, which applies to campaigns as well. Campaigns that try to chase every moving object usually end up wasting limited resources without reaching their ultimate goal. It is a simple truth that if everything is a priority, then nothing is a priority.

A clear targeting strategy allows you to adapt your message to what your audience wants to hear.[13] In an election campaign, you do not have to please everyone. Polarization and conflict might even be helpful in attracting media attention and creating voter engagement. The key is that your target audience really loves what you have to say.

A great example was Donald Trump when he first ran for president in 2016. Journalists, pundits, and commentators were appalled by some of the things he said, but his supporters loved not only what he said but also how he said it.

That being said, there are basically three ways to target voters:

1. *You can target voters geographically.* In US presidential elections, for example, the so-called swing states are crucially important. If you live in Pennsylvania or Florida, you'll see television ads from the presidential candidates during each and every commercial break. On the other hand, if you live in California, which hasn't voted for a Republican presidential candidate since Ronald Reagan, you may never see a presidential campaign ad. In many other countries, there is a political dividing line between north and south or east and west of the country. It often goes along with cleavages regarding language, ethnicity, religion, or standard of living. The cleavage between rural and urban areas has also grown to become one of the most important dividing lines in many countries.
2. *You can target voters ideologically.* This means that a campaign is trying to reach conservatives, liberals, socialists, Christian conservatives, or another group. This also includes targeting voters who care about a certain issue, whether it is abortion, taxes, or gun ownership.
3. *You can target voters sociodemographically.* The most common criteria for this are gender, age, race, educational background, and income. In the US, for example, a majority of white voters backed the Republican candidate for president in 2020, while minority voters overwhelmingly voted for the Democratic one. According to the CNN exit polls (see Targeting Coalitions table), 58 percent of white

voters voted for Donald Trump, while 41 percent of them voted for Joe Biden. On the other hand, Biden won 87 percent of black and 65 percent of Latino voters, compared to 12 percent and 32 percent respectively for Trump. The gap becomes even more pronounced once education is added to the equation. According to the CNN exit polls again, 67 percent of white voters without a college degree voted for Trump, while only 32 percent of them voted for Biden. The gender gap has also been talked about a lot: 57 percent of female voters went for Biden, and 42 percent for Trump. It is almost the reverse among men: 53 percent of male voters backed Trump, while 45 percent voted for Biden. It's further interesting to look at race and gender together. 61 percent of white men voted for Trump, 38 percent for Biden. Among white women, 55 percent voted for Trump while 44 percent voted for Biden. 79 percent of black men and 90 percent of black women voted for Biden, while 19 percent of black men and 9 percent of black women voted for Trump.[14]

TARGETING COALITIONS

	Male (%) (48)	Female (%) (52)
Biden	45	57
Trump	53	42

	White (%) (67)	Black (%) (13)	Latino (%) (13)	Asian (%) (4)	Other (%) (4)
Biden	41	87	65	61	55
Trump	58	12	32	34	41

	White Men (%) (35)	White Women (%) (32)	Black Men (%) (4)	Black Women (%) (8)	Latino Men (%) (5)	Latino Women (%) (8)	All Other Races (%) (8)
Biden	38	44	79	90	59	69	58
Trump	61	55	19	9	36	30	38

	White Voters, College Degree (%) (32)	White Voters, No College Degree (%) (35)	Voters of Color, College Degree (%) (10)	Voters of Color, No College Degree (%) (24)
Biden	51	32	70	72
Trump	48	67	27	26

Source: "Exit Polls," *CNN*, accessed April 28, 2023, https://edition.cnn.com/election/2020/exit-polls/president/national-results.

In most campaigns, there is a mix between geographic, ideological, and sociodemographic targeting. Your own mix will depend a lot on the sociodemographic structure of your area, the political cleavages, and the information you have available. In some countries, there is much less data on voters available than in the US, which limits the toolkit at your disposal. Whatever your targeting strategy will be, it will then have to be translated into specific measures. You have to think about which media outlets, publications, and channels are the best way to reach your targets. If you target rural voters, you can buy billboards in rural areas, run ads on rural radio stations, try to get into papers that have high circulation in rural areas, and plan campaign events and activities in rural areas. If you target voters who care a lot about climate change, then you will first of all have to offer an appealing and substantive message on the issue, which you will then promote in publications that these voters read. You can try to find or buy a list of voters who care about environmental issues and try to get the endorsements of environmental groups. If you target young voters, you can run ads in commercial breaks during TV shows that young people watch. You get the gist. After a baseline survey, you will ideally run a tracking survey in which you can then assess the progress you made among each of your target groups.

HOW TO DEVELOP A WINNING MESSAGE FOR A CHALLENGER

I strongly believe that words matter in politics. It has been said that "politics is the mastery of words." Regardless of what candidates are saying, the mere choice of their words already communicates their priorities and values to voters. If you care about the middle class or about small business, for example, use these words in your speeches. Once you know how many voters you need to win over and you have a targeting strategy defining who these potential voters are, you then need to decide what your campaign will communicate to those target voters. Or put differently, what will be your message?

When I talk about message, many candidates and politicians think about a tagline or a slogan. It's more than that, and much work goes into it. Dr. Ronald Faucheux, the professor I mentioned earlier, defined the message as the reason why voters should vote for your side and not the other side (or one of the other sides). Many campaigns, unfortunately, never explicitly formulate a message in that sense, and it's a big mistake. What I first learned from Faucheux about message development has inspired my work around the globe during the past twenty years and several things I write in this chapter. While the message may never be published as such, it's the basis for all communication of a campaign. Every speech, press release, ad, and visual should communicate at least a part of your message.

Here are some examples from recent US presidential elections. In 2012, when incumbent president Barack Obama was running for reelection against Mitt Romney, his message went like this:

> Four years ago, the US faced the most dramatic financial crisis since the Great Depression. Since then, we are on the way to

> recovery. We rescued the US auto industry and killed Osama bin Laden. Mitt Romney, on the other hand, is a cold capitalist who has made a fortune out of outsourcing. He does not understand average people and wants to go back to the failed policies of the past that got us into the crisis in the first place. We have come too far to turn back now. Let us move forward!

In 2016, when Donald Trump was the challenger who ran against Hillary Clinton, his message was the following:

> Donald Trump is not one of the many career politicians in Washington, DC. Instead, he has built a successful multibillion-dollar business. This background makes Trump the right person to bring much-needed change. He will help the forgotten middle class by protecting our borders and negotiating new trade deals. Crooked Hillary has been in politics for thirty years. With her, it is all talk and no action. Donald Trump will make America safe and great again.

In 2020, Joe Biden's message running against incumbent Donald Trump went like this:

> Donald Trump's handling of COVID-19 is the biggest failure of any American president in history. After 220,000 deaths and eight million cases, Donald Trump still does not have a convincing plan for how to deal with this pandemic. Joe Biden will follow scientific advice to master this crisis, to reopen and rebuild the country. Joe Biden will bring decency and honor back to the White House and reunite and heal America.

As these examples illustrate, a good message is first of all short and understandable. While important intellectual work goes into message development, keep things simple. You and your campaign team should do that brain work, not the voters. To put it in plain English, the least educated voter in your constituency should be able to understand it, so this is not the place to show off how smart you are.

The campaign message is of course inspired by the political conviction of the candidate, but it's much shorter than a party platform. In fact, it's a concise summary of what the candidate stands for, applied to the current situation. In political marketing, we often use the concepts of political demand (public opinion) and political offer (your message). The key to a successful campaign is that your message is in sync with the political demand of your target audience. In other words, what you consider to be the important message is not necessarily what your target audience cares about. I remember a conversation I had with a vice president who planned to run for president of his country. In a talk we had years before the campaign began, he told me that he already knew his slogan, "wisdom and experience," which he thought would perfectly summarize his record and biography. In fairness to the vice president, it did, but unfortunately, wisdom and experience was not what the electorate looked for in that election. Your message should therefore be something that is relevant to the daily lives of your target audience and offers a solution to issues they care about. Unfortunately, many campaigns fail that simple benchmark in their message development because they are driven by ideology or plain righteousness.

Another typical beginner's mistake made by campaign teams when formulating a message is that they confuse it with something that in the corporate world would serve as a mission statement. A mission statement answers the question of "who we are" in broad and general terms, when a message for an election campaign needs much more urgency. Why vote for my side *this time*?

In that sense, a good message is a coherent narrative. The examples above illustrate what this means: a good story usually has a villain, a victim, a hero—and it has conflict and dialogue. If you think about past US presidential campaigns, isn't it also telling that most people would have a difficult time recalling the message of Hillary Clinton or Mitt Romney in a similarly catchy way?

Message development doesn't happen in a vacuum but has a lot to do with showing contrast with your opponent. Think about the biggest weaknesses of your opponent. What do voters dislike the most about your opponent? Then try to showcase the opposite in a credible way. This is sometimes difficult to fully comprehend for marketing and advertising professionals who are used to promoting products. Consumers do not have to decide once every four years whether they want to buy Kit Kat or M&M's. They can avail of both or choose one today and the other one tomorrow. As a result, advertising for consumer products often consists of long-term branding campaigns. Imagine for a moment how their advertising would change if consumers had to decide one day whether to drink Coca-Cola or Pepsi for the next four years. They would probably work out the difference between the two much more explicitly.

Joe Biden's campaign in 2020 is a good illustration. At the time, COVID-19 was dominating the news, and one thing the Biden campaign did well was to capitalize on the issue. Biden drew contrast by acknowledging the importance of the virus and by underlining his willingness to follow the advice of scientific experts. In addition, the difference between the two candidates was also shown with respect to form when Biden radically changed his campaign style, moved everything online, made it a point to always wear a mask, and constantly respected social distancing in his rare public appearances. On the other side, Donald Trump at first was reluctant to wear a mask and seemed to downplay the gravity of the situation (at least in public). Toward the end of the campaign, Trump himself, the First Lady, and several others from Trump's inner circle tested positive for the virus. This painted the picture of the White House as a COVID-19 hot spot, and the distinction between his and Biden's campaign could not have been clearer.

While the examples I gave you are all from US presidential elections, message development is key for any campaign, at any level of government, and in any country. In a two-party system, voters have only two options, and as a result, contrast is shown explicitly and the opponent addressed directly. In a system with several candidates or parties, contrast is shown more implicitly, and of course, cultural differences are also important here. I have done a lot of work in various Asian and European countries, and most candidates would not be as harsh about their opponents as in the examples above. But the principle remains the same. Whether you run for senator in Brazil, *conseil général* in France's Poitou-Charentes, or president of Indonesia, you need to give voters a reason to vote for you.

For a challenger or opposition campaign, the generic, natural message is that the country, state, or city is on the wrong track and that change—in particular a change in leadership—is urgently needed. The incumbent, on the other hand, will say that things are going well and that the country, state, or city should continue that route of progress and prosperity with the same leadership.

When Bill Clinton ran for president and challenged incumbent George H. W. Bush, he used classic challenger rhetoric. In his speech at the party convention, when he accepted the nomination and officially became the presidential candidate of the Democratic Party, he said this, for example:

> So, if you are sick and tired of a government that doesn't work to create jobs, if you're sick and tired of a tax system that's stacked against you, if you're sick and tired of exploding debt and reduced investment in our future, or if, like the great civil rights pioneer Fannie Lou Hamer, you're just plain old sick and tired of being sick and tired, then join us, work with us,

> win with us, and we can make our country the country it was meant to be.

In the same speech, he gave voters a reason to vote for change now:

> We meet at a special moment in history, you and I. The Cold War is over. Soviet communism has collapsed and our values [...] have triumphed all around the world. And yet, just as we have won the Cold War abroad, we are losing the battles for economic opportunity and social justice here at home. Now that we have changed the world, it's time to change America. I have news for the forces of greed and the defenders of the status quo: Your time has come and gone. It's time for a change in America.[15]

While Clinton's speech is a great case of challenger discourse, calling for change is not reserved to politicians from the left of the political spectrum. Opposition candidates from the right also successfully claim and campaign on change, as George W. Bush and Donald Trump did in the US. In Spain as well, Mariano Rajoy successfully campaigned with the slogan *súmate al cambio* (join the change). More than a decade earlier, José María Aznar defeated the socialist incumbent with a sober call for change, *con la nueva mayoría* (with the new majority). In the UK, David Cameron from the Conservative Party successfully challenged incumbent Gordon Brown from the Labour Party with "vote for change."

If a majority of voters truly are unhappy with the status quo, it is important to actively tie the status quo to the incumbent candidate. You have to make sure the incumbent's policies and decisions are perceived as the cause of the discontent about the status quo. It's important not to let the incumbent blame something or someone else for it. You also shouldn't sound like you're criticizing the country and its people. Voters don't like to hear that. In your communication, it should be clear that the incumbent is the problem, not the country. A great example of this is when François Hollande challenged incumbent Nicolas Sarkozy to become president of France in 2012. Hollande literally prosecuted Sarkozy by making statements such as "this is not a record, it's a fiasco."[16] This was after the financial crisis and the economy and purchasing power were the main issues for voters. Hollande made sure Sarkozy could not use the financial crisis as an excuse for the state of things. In almost every public statement, he tried to pin down the incumbent by naming key decisions the incumbent made before and after the financial crisis.

Of all the possible ways to tie an incumbent to the status quo, we can boil them down to the following suggestions:

- expose how the incumbent refuses to acknowledge the problem
- demonstrate that the incumbent does not understand the problem (so how can he be part of the solution?)
- show that the incumbent has ignored facts and warning signs that led to the current situation
- point out that the incumbent refuses to take responsibility or tries to blame others
- create urgency (give people a reason to change now)
- emphasize the risk of inaction (what happens if the incumbent continues for four more years?).

Sometimes, the sheer duration of the incumbent leadership can be an argument for change in itself. The longer an incumbent has been in power, the more the thirst of the public for a change in leadership grows. When Vicente Fox ran for president of Mexico, for example, the incumbent Institutional Revolutionary Party, *Partido Revolucionario Institucional* (PRI), had been in power for more than seventy years. Getting rid of the incumbent party was key to Fox's strategy to put together a broad coalition that disagreed on many things but had a common purpose in ending the incumbent regime.

A question we often ask in surveys is whether people want a continuation of the incumbent's direction, or if they prefer a new direction. If the results to that question are clear cut, which is often the case, then the consequences for the messaging are obvious. If voters are mixed and have not closed the door on the incumbent, you have to adapt and soften your call for change. In such a situation, it might be better to offer improvement in key areas rather than change. I once worked for a candidate where the answer to the question of whether or not voters wanted to continue the direction of the incumbent was exactly a split—half of the electorate wanted to continue while the other half wanted a change. This was tricky for the positioning strategy of my client. We solved this by saying that our candidate would continue the programs a majority of voters liked from the incumbent, while clearly showing contrast regarding the things voters disliked about the incumbent.

In other situations, an incumbent's relatively high job approval rating might hide an underlying weakness that can be exploited. I was once hired to help a candidate challenge the incumbent mayor of a big city. In the survey, I found that 75 percent of the voters thought that the city was going in the right direction and the incumbent mayor had a favorability rating of 65 percent. When we asked in the survey who they would vote for, less than two months before the election, we trailed the incumbent 39 percent to 50 percent. The focus groups revealed, however, that the high job approval rating was mostly fueled by the projects the incumbent had implemented. Especially with respect to the personality of the incumbent mayor, voters had quite negative things to say. While they saw and appreciated some of the mayor's accomplishments, they disliked the person. He was perceived as partisan and as someone who was always looking for fights. I therefore advised my principal to present himself as warm and respectful.

He needed to make it clear that if elected mayor, his social services would be for everyone, not based on favoritism. In addition, I advised him on how to talk about the issues that were of most pressing concern to voters and on how to neutralize some of his own weaknesses. I will never forget the session where I presented the results and my recommendations because at the end of it, the candidate was given a bulletproof vest. On election day, he beat the incumbent mayor 51 percent to 47 percent.

I mentioned earlier that as a teenager, I was active in the youth organization of a party. At a convention, I remember how the national party chairman told me that usually one big issue ultimately decides the outcome of an election. He was absolutely right, and in many instances, that dominating issue relates to the state of the economy, whether it's unemployment, inflation, or poverty in general. When COVID-19 hit, however, the pandemic became the dominant issue overnight. In other cases, it can be an international crisis, a geopolitical question, or the environment, to name a few. Whatever the dominant issue is, you have to show that it is not going well because of the incumbent's decisions or lack thereof. In addition to that, you also have to show that you can do better. In other words, you have to build up credibility on the issue.

Opposition candidates always think of themselves as having the right answers for the issues in question, but if they lose, it's often because voters disagree. Issue ownership has become particularly important nowadays as voters are increasingly cynical about their political leaders. I have long witnessed this during my work in developing countries where, by and large, average voters think that all politicians are corrupt and will not even try to keep their election promises. I now observe the same trend in the Western world. It is no longer enough to have a message and to talk about it. As a campaign, you need an entire communication plan to make your message believable. For example, if you plan to run on the economy, then you should have, say, a five-point plan for economic recovery. You should be surrounded and endorsed by known and esteemed economic leaders. It would also be helpful if you could portray to voters how you have handled (economic) turnaround situations earlier in your career. In short, there needs to be meat on the bone.

In order for it to be believable for voters, the message also has to be consistent over time. In that respect, I remember the 1995 presidential campaign of Édouard Balladur in France. Balladur represented an antiquated vision of France and was the opposite of change. When it became clear that voters were looking for change—a claim his main opponent had campaigned on for months—he started to propose "change in continuity." It lacked all credibility.

LAST PIECE OF ADVICE

Developing your campaign message also includes deciding what you will *not* say and what the campaign message will not be about. Ideally, you avoid campaigning on an issue that your side is divided on. If your own party is split, how can voters be convinced you have the right plan? Furthermore, your message should not include issues, topics, and character traits that your opponent is more known for than you are yourself. This often feels counterintuitive to clients. Especially when a candidate feels vulnerable and defensive about an issue, the reflex is to insist even more that you are right. In this case, the intuition is wrong and makes things worse. You should campaign on issues that work in your favor. Bill Clinton, for example, praised George H. W. Bush for his foreign policy because Clinton wanted to campaign on the economy. Therefore, remember that agreeing with your opponent about issues that they're strongest on will help focus the campaign and increase contrast on the matter that you want the campaign to be about.

3

THE BEST CHALLENGER CAMPAIGN MESSAGING EVER

The greatest challenger campaign ever was when Barack Obama ran for president in 2008. In this chapter, I want to explain why I think so and what other opposition candidates can learn from the case, with a particular focus on message and strategy development.

At the time, Republican George W. Bush approached the end of his second term in the White House, and Senator John McCain, a decorated war hero, was nominated as the Republican standard-bearer. On the side of the Democrats, Hillary Clinton, the former First Lady and senator from New York, was seen as the front-runner for the nomination. But another Democrat, Barack Obama, junior senator from Illinois, threw his hat into the ring. He first won an upset victory in the Democratic primaries against Hillary Clinton and then went on to win the general election against John McCain.

During the primaries, the Obama team focused for many months on Iowa, the first state to vote. The candidate and his strategists concluded that if they had any chance to challenge the front-runner,

Hillary Clinton, they needed a surprisingly good result in the early states. This sounds obvious in hindsight, but David Plouffe, Obama's campaign manager, shared with me in an interview for this book that, at the time, they paid a heavy price for their targeting strategy. Concentrating on Iowa, whose electorate consisted predominantly of white voters, de facto meant not to pay much attention to the African American community. As a consequence, the nationwide survey numbers didn't move for a long time, and Obama was trailing Clinton badly. The candidate in particular was under pressure from donors and the media to change course but continued to carry out the plan with discipline.[17] This paid off as Obama won Iowa and, after a long fight, the Democratic nomination.

During the general election, the Obama team again focused like a laser on reaching 270 electoral votes, which is needed to win a US presidential election. I don't want to get into the details of the electoral system at this point, but the team understood that it's not enough to simply get more votes than the competition—they had to get them in the right states.

The campaign team was again disciplined with respect to its targeting strategy. A winning Obama coalition for the general election included overwhelming support from African Americans, two-thirds of Hispanics, and a sizable minority, about 40 percent, of white voters.

With respect to the message, Obama's entire campaign was built on one central tagline: "change." The overall campaign message went like this:

> Barack Obama will bring the change that America desperately needs. He will get the economy going again, not only for Wall Street but also for Main Street. In concrete, this means tax cuts for 95 percent of Americans and expanded health care. John McCain, on the other hand, will continue the war in Iraq and

> the failed policies of George Bush. It is time for a new hope and to leave the divisiveness behind us. Yes, we can!

This message was the basis for the campaign's advertising and the candidate's speeches. At the Democratic National Convention where Obama accepted the nomination, for example, he framed the election as a choice between change and more of the same:

> The same party that brought you two terms of George Bush and Dick Cheney will ask this country for a third. And we are here because we love this country too much to let the next four years look like the last eight. On November 4, we must stand up and say: "Eight is enough."[18]

And he actively tied the incumbent government to the status quo:

> These challenges are not all of government's making. But the failure to respond is a direct result of a broken politics in Washington and the failed policies of George W. Bush. America, we are better than these last eight years.[19]

Some people at the time thought that Obama's claim of hope and change was merely a slogan empty of content, but I strongly disagree. The purpose of a campaign slogan is to summarize the message with oomph, and Obama's slogan accomplished that. In my conversation with David Plouffe, we also discussed how the campaign had tested various slogans. It ultimately decided on "change we can believe in," which was long but drove the point home during the primaries. During the general election, it became "change we need." In both cases, it was important to show contrast and showcase that Obama really meant what he said. "Change itself was not enough, people always hear that," Plouffe told me.[20]

The internal research of the Obama campaign revealed an important point in that respect, namely that voters believed that Obama himself truly wanted change. They also thought that someone who was relatively new to politics would be more likely to make change happen than a longtime career politician. This was an important finding because Obama had only served a bit more than two years in the US Senate by the time he announced his run for president. With the focus on change, the team could turn a potential weakness into a strength.[21]

In an internal survey, Obama led McCain on who would bring fundamental change in the way Washington does business 40 percent to 18 percent. The campaign also tested a series of what they called "essential change attributes" and found that they were leading McCain on all of them. When voters were asked which one of the two candidates would put partisan politics aside to get things done, Obama was leading McCain 42 percent to 30 percent. Regarding the question which candidate would tell people what they *needed* to hear instead of what they *wanted* to hear, Obama led McCain 39 percent to 36 percent. With respect to which candidate would put the needs of working- and middle-class Americans ahead of special interests and big corporations, Obama led McCain 46 percent to 20 percent.[22]

Equally important to Obama's promise was the consistency of his message. The same key elements can be found in his announcement speech, his address at the Democratic National Convention, and the victory speech on election night. The message never changed much.

In our discussions, Plouffe also revealed to me how they vigorously defended their territory against McCain. "We spent a lot of time on making sure McCain would not be seen as an outsider insurgent," says David Plouffe. It is important to remember that at least in political circles, McCain was known as a maverick who would occasionally defy his own party. He had worked across the aisle with Democrats in the Senate to get legislation passed on key issues such as campaign finance reform. Among the potential Republican candidates at the time, McCain was best positioned to run a campaign that would be independent from the Republican establishment and from incumbent president George W. Bush, who had become very unpopular by that time. At the Republican National Convention, when McCain officially became the candidate, he was indeed presented to the public as an agent of change. In its internal research, though, the Obama campaign found that the broader electorate did not know much about McCain's past as a maverick. This was an important finding because it allowed the campaign to tie McCain to incumbent Bush and frame a vote for McCain as a vote for a third term for Bush.

During the primaries, McCain was competing against other Republicans who challenged him from the right. McCain defended himself by saying in an interview that he had voted with Bush 90 percent of the time—more than many of his Republican colleagues. In the general election, the Obama campaign used that footage and produced an ad called "90 Percent." The ad included pictures of Bush and McCain and showed McCain speaking in his own words about his support for incumbent Bush. It also attacked McCain for supporting "tax breaks for big corporations and the wealthy, but almost nothing for the middle class. Same as Bush. Keep spending $10 billion a month in Iraq while our own economy struggles? Same as Bush."[23]

In sync with the advertising, candidate Obama pushed the same message in his campaign speeches. At a rally, candidate Obama ridiculed McCain:

> I guess his whole angle is, "Watch out, George Bush—except for economic policy, health care policy, tax policy, education policy, foreign policy and Karl Rove-style politics—we're really going to shake things up in Washington."[24]

In other words, the Obama campaign was not hesitant to draw lines of distinction between Obama and McCain. Even if they were running against an accomplished war hero, they would go on the offense in the right tone. As an example, McCain campaigned on the slogan "country first," and in his acceptance speech Obama attacked it head-on, but by using patriotic rhetoric:

> The times are too serious, the stakes are too high for this same partisan playbook. So let us agree that patriotism has no party. I love this country, and so do you, and so does John McCain. The men and women who serve in our battlefields may be Democrats and Republicans and independents, but they have fought together and bled together, and some died together under the same proud flag. They have not served a red America or a blue America—they have served the United States of America. So I've got news for you, John McCain. We all put our country first.[25]

The Obama campaign also used the sheer duration of McCain's time in Washington, DC, in order to define him as more of the same. McCain was portrayed as a man of the past who could not possibly be an agent of change as he claimed to be. One ad called "Still" went as follows:

> 1982. John McCain goes to Washington. Things have changed in the last twenty-six years [images appear of old telephones and computers]. But, McCain hasn't. He admits he still doesn't know how to use a computer. Can't send an e-mail. Still doesn't understand the economy and favors $200 billion in new tax cuts for corporations, but almost nothing for the middle class. After one president who was out of touch, we just can't afford

> more of the same [a picture appears of John McCain together with George Bush].[26]

There was no doubt that Obama offered change. The challenge for his campaign was to ensure that they did not frighten voters by offering too much change. In his campaign speeches, Obama tried to neutralize himself against attacks that the campaign assumed would come in one form or another. In his acceptance speech at the Democratic National Convention, he said the following:

> Because if you don't have any fresh ideas, then you use stale tactics to scare the voters. If you don't have a record to run on, then you paint your opponent as someone people should run from.[27]

On the stump, he spoke similarly:

> So nobody really thinks that Bush or McCain have the real answer for the challenges we face, so what they're going to try to do is make you scared of me. You know, he's not patriotic enough. He's got a funny name. You know, he doesn't look like all those other presidents on those dollar bills, you know. He's risky.[28]

In order to make voters comfortable to vote for Obama, the candidate emphasized his middle-class background. Obama also embarked on a trip abroad to seven countries, including Israel and a visit to American troops in Iraq and Afghanistan. It was meant to showcase to the electorate at home that he was able to act on the world stage and be commander in chief. The trip was successful as, months later, respondents in the focus groups still mentioned it positively. Another key component in Obama's reassuring strategy was the selection of

Joe Biden as his vice presidential candidate. In many ways, Biden was the antithesis of Obama. He was an elder white man who had spent decades in the Senate. The rationale was that a Washington, DC insider such as Biden would help Obama implement the change he was promising.

With respect to specific issues, voters were mostly concerned about the economy, and they desired a president who could get it moving again. At the outset of the campaign, however, it wasn't an issue that allowed either candidate to stand out as an expert. An early survey showed that Obama led McCain on "who could best fix the economy" 32 percent to 19 percent.[29]

Obama himself also worried that their own advertising was not clear and strong enough on the issue of the economy.[30] He wanted his team to sharpen the message and to show a more distinct contrast with his Republican opponent.[31] Among other things, the campaign decided to produce a two-minute TV ad that would feature Obama talking straight into the camera. The two-minute duration alone is remarkable in itself for a political ad. I have experienced myself several times that candidates don't want to run commercials that are longer than thirty seconds because of the heavy cost. In the two-minute ad, Obama detailed an economic plan that included tax breaks for the middle class, stricter regulation of Wall Street, energy independence, and a crackdown on lobbyists.[32] Even after seeing it several times, few TV watchers probably remembered the details of the plan, but given the long format and the detailed communication it allowed, the ad conveyed to voters that Obama in fact did have a plan.

This would soon be of great value, as on September 15, 2008, the financial services firm Lehman Brothers filed for bankruptcy.[33] At the time of writing, this remains the biggest bankruptcy filing in US history and marked the catalyst of what later became known as the subprime mortgage crisis. It was a tremendous shock to the financial system, and, by its sheer magnitude, the bankruptcy went beyond usual current events that are always impacting an ongoing election campaign. Overnight, the menacing collapse of the financial system and its implications for the entire economy became the number one issue. Conventional wisdom has it that the Obama campaign benefited electorally from the banking meltdown, and I agree, it probably did. I do not think that this was an automatic, guaranteed result. At a time of such a crisis, voters could have also preferred a more senior statesman. The outcome—that Obama was ultimately seen as more trustworthy to navigate through the crisis despite having less experience than McCain—was the product of key decisions the two campaigns made.

On the day the bankruptcy was announced, McCain happened to campaign in Jacksonville, Florida, and told the audience that he believed that the fundamentals of the economy were strong. "Our economy, I think still—the fundamentals of our economy are strong," McCain apparently read from a prepared transcript.[34] To make that statement on the day when the markets tanked and the entire financial and banking system seemed in peril made McCain look as though he did not grasp the seriousness of the situation. The statement was also damaging to McCain because it was part of a bigger pattern. During the primary campaign, McCain had said that economics was not something he understood as well as he should have.[35] Those were statements that the Obama campaign could and did use against the Republican nominee. Instead of trying to build up more economic competence and compete for the ownership of the issue, McCain committed more gaffes. In a television interview, McCain appeared not to know exactly how many houses he owned.[36] On another occasion, McCain said that the dividing line between rich and middle class was maybe a yearly income of five million dollars.[37] One of those statements would have been possible for McCain to defend, but the problem for him was that there was a pattern emerging. He appeared out of touch with economic realities and rather thin on substance on the matter.

Meanwhile, Obama skillfully took advantage of McCain's mishandling of the situation when he said this:

> It's not that I think John McCain doesn't care what's going on in the lives of most Americans. I just think he doesn't know. Why else would he say, today, of all days, just a few hours ago, that the fundamentals of our economy are strong? Senator, what economy are you talking about?[38]

In addition to having the right message, David Plouffe has highlighted for me how important it also is to have the right attitude. "Challengers are often seen as the underdog and you therefore need a fighting spirit, that you're gonna stick to your plan and do this," Plouffe stated.[39] It's often that mindset—that you have nothing to lose—that is crucial for a win. When it was all said and done, and after executing their strategy almost flawlessly, Obama beat McCain 52.9 percent to 45.7 percent. In the all-important Electoral College, Obama won 365 electoral votes compared with 173 for McCain, far more than the 270 needed to win the White House.[40]

4

THE SECRETS OF SELLING CHANGE

Even when large segments of the electorate are unhappy with the status quo, change is nevertheless frightening for some voters. If you think about it from their perspective, there is no guarantee that a change in leadership will make things better. In fact, change could also make things worse. I remember a voter in a caucus who compared voting for a challenger to moving: "Yes, you are unhappy with the current house, but you also want to know what the new house will look like." In that sense, you must convince voters that moving is worth the effort and will result in a real improvement. In this chapter, we discuss what that means when translated to electoral politics—in other words, the strategies and tactics needed to make voters comfortable to vote for change.

In many countries, politics has become awfully polarized, and as a result, party leaders are increasingly appealing to their base—rather than reaching out to undecided voters—to win elections. In some cases, politicians have literally become prisoners of their own party faithful, and any centrism is seen as treason. The present chapter is of particular importance to them because sometimes they forget that despite an obvious trend toward polarization, there are still undecided and swing voters. They are often in the political center, and while there are fewer of them than there were ten or twenty years ago, they are in many instances the ones to decide an election.

Change should usually be defined as a change in leadership, fresh faces, an improved economy, and implementing important reforms. Most voters around the world are skeptical about change rooted in ideology, such as the introduction of radical new policies or an abrupt change in values. I remember I once discussed this with a congressman client of mine. After many years in office, he faced a challenge that was more formidable than those in his past. We ran some focus groups and the bottom line was clear. "I think voters are looking for improvement, not radical change," my client correctly summarized. It was a good thing for us that the challenger did not know that and campaigned on a tagline of fundamental change. While the challenger had an opening with voters at the beginning of the campaign, his offer was a mismatch with where public opinion stood. Yes, revolutions sometimes do happen, but they usually take place against autocratic regimes. In this book, I am writing about democratic elections, and in most of these cases, voters want to be assured that change will not be all too radical. In that sense, voters are often looking for what marketing experts call "a permission structure," meaning that they are looking for reassurance that the risk in voting for change is manageable. I will now describe some of the most effective strategies and tactics to accomplish that.

SHOWCASE SUCCESSFUL GOVERNMENT RECORD AT THE LOCAL LEVEL

Successful challengers often have prior experience at the local level. One of the best strategies to make voters comfortable to embrace the change you are offering is therefore to show what you have done effectively on a smaller scale. "Look what we have done in our province or state; what we are proposing are not empty promises or partisan ideology" is the message. At the time of writing, the presidents of Mexico, Indonesia, and the Philippines and the chancellor of Germany, to name a few, are former governors and mayors. In the US, Jimmy Carter, Ronald Reagan, Bill Clinton, and George W. Bush all served as governors before becoming president. Clinton, for example, used his record as governor of Arkansas when he challenged incumbent president George H. W. Bush. When he accepted the nomination at the Democratic National Convention, he asked rhetorically, "How do I know we can come together and make change happen? Because I have seen it in my own state. In Arkansas, we are working together, and we are making progress." And in particular on the issue of budgetary discipline, he said this: "He [the incumbent] has never balanced a government budget, but I have eleven times."[41] That's powerful rhetoric!

NEUTRALIZE HISTORIC WEAKNESS ON A SPECIFIC ISSUE

Parties (and politicians who run under their banner) often have clear, historically grown strengths and weaknesses. For example, progressive, leftist parties are generally considered to deliver on social issues and social justice, the welfare state, pensions, and education. Their vulnerabilities usually include immigration, budgetary discipline, taxes, and crime. For conservative parties it's quite the opposite. They are at times seen as delivering with respect to immigration, safety, and the economy. Their weaknesses, on the other hand, are often that they are perceived not to care much about social justice or the environment. If your party has been in opposition for some time, then it is likely that one of the reasons is what we call a policy disagreement, meaning that the solution your party offers on a key issue is not in sync with what a majority of voters want regarding the matter in question. There are various ways to deal with this, but the first step is to acknowledge it internally and decide on a new path moving forward. Politicians on the left often think that voters are simply stupid not to appreciate their solutions. Politicians on the right tend to blame the media, suggesting that all journalists are leftists, and if only the candidates were to get fair coverage, voters would understand their solutions. Neither are effective ways of dealing with a policy disagreement because you are giving away the keys to change the situation. Here are two other suggestions for a more proactive approach:

- Adopt the policy of your opponent: there is nothing wrong with learning in politics and with absorbing new information as the world evolves. It is good to have values, and I'm certainly not advocating to flip-flop on every issue as the winds are changing. If the policy disagreement has been going on for years or sometimes even decades, however, there is a possibility that the other side is right. In the Western world, for example, I think that most conservative parties would fare better if they were to be more vocal about the environment. And most progressive parties, on the other hand, would resonate more with voters if they were less ideological about immigration. Of course, such a change of policy cannot be done overnight but has to be carried out in a credible way over a certain period of time.
- Try to explain your position better: if you don't want to change your position and you are sure that you are right, then you have to make an effort to explain it better. A good example of this is the 1981 French presidential election when François Mitterrand challenged incumbent Valéry Giscard d'Estaing. One of the issues at the time was the abolition of the death penalty. In a televised debate, Mitterrand explained why he opposed the death penalty, knowing full well that a majority of French people were in favor of it:

> It is my deep conviction, together with the churches [...] and the totality of the national and international humanitarian organizations, that I am against the death penalty. And I don't need the surveys to tell me that a majority of the voters are for capital punishment. I'm running for president, I'm asking for a majority of the votes, but I'm not asking for it in the secrecy of my thinking. I'm telling you what I think, what I believe, what my spiritual adhesions are, and my concern for civilization.*

Voters respect someone with convictions. If explained well, they will forgive a policy disagreement even on a major issue. This strategy, however, can only be used selectively. You can't be out of sync with the majority position on several issues.

CANDIDATES MORE MODERATE THAN THEIR OWN PARTY STAND A BETTER CHANCE TO WIN

As mentioned at the beginning of this chapter, politics in many countries has become divisive. While there is nothing wrong with party activists having strong convictions, successful challengers usually need to build broader coalitions between their party faithful and more centrist and independent swing voters. As a result, successful opposition

* "Dans ma conscience profonde, qui rejoint celle des églises, l'église catholique, les églises réformées, la religion juive, la totalité des grandes associations humanitaires, internationales, et nationales, dans ma conscience, dans le for de ma conscience, je suis contre la peine de mort. Et, je n'ai pas besoin de lire les sondages, qui disent le contraire. Une opinion majoritaire est pour la peine de mort. Eh bien moi, je suis candidat à la Présidence de la République, et je demande une majorité de suffrages aux Français, mais je ne la demande pas dans le secret de ma pensée. Je dis ce que je pense, ce à quoi j'adhère, ce à quoi je crois, ce à quoi se rattachent mes adhésions spirituelles, ma croyance, mon souci de la civilisation." "François Mitterrand se prononce contre la peine de mort," INA, March 16, 1981, https://fresques.ina.fr/mitterrand/fiche-media/Mitter00030/francois-mitterrand-se-prononce-contre-la-peine-de-mort.html.

candidates often maintain some ideological distance from their own party. A typical tactic for top candidates is to write a book about their vision. As it is their book, and not a party platform that needs to be adopted by the party, it allows them to position themselves more in the center than their own party. Another tactic is to talk about who you would appoint to your cabinet if elected and to name moderate people or well-respected experts in their fields.

A great example of a centrist positioning strategy is David Cameron, who was first the leader of the Conservative Party in Britain, then later served as prime minister. When Cameron threw his hat into the ring to become the leader of his party, he gave a key speech at the party convention that literally propelled his candidacy. In the speech, he energized the party faithful but also reached out far into the political center. The speech is in many ways a great illustration of the model presented in this book. To begin with, Cameron used the word "change" eight times during his speech and the word "new" ten times. Yes, using the right words with repetition matters in politics. He proposed a modern, compassionate conservatism, fueling a country that "engages enthusiastically with the wider world" and a party that is "comfortable with modern Britain." He also urged his own party to change: "we've got to change our culture so we look, feel, think and behave like a completely new organization." In addition to such great challenger rhetoric, he made key statements to underline his stance. Margaret Thatcher, the longtime Conservative prime minister and a tremendously important figure of the party, had famously said that there was no such thing as society. Cameron took this statement head-on and said that "there is such a thing as society; it's just not the same thing as the state." With respect to issues, Cameron spent much time in his speech on education. While the Conservatives traditionally stood for less government, lower taxes, and being tough on crime, education was not an issue they were strong on. Cameron, nevertheless, spoke at length about it and used it as a signature topic to illustrate how he intended to reposition his party. After that, he even went a step further and declared, "we'll share—that's right, we'll share—the fruits of economic growth between tax reduction and public services." He then continued: "Yes, the Conservative Party understands that the quality of life matters as well as the quantity of money."[42] The commitment must have been stunning to hear for many conservative convention attendees.

When Cameron finished his speech, which, to a large extent, sounded more progressive than conservative, the delegates erupted in applause and rose for a standing ovation. You might wonder, why did his party not only accept Cameron's approach but embrace it and ultimately elect him as their leader? Because they were also tired of losing three elections in a row, and Cameron was able to convince them that his approach would lead them to power after more than a decade in the opposition. In that sense, a key sentence spoken by Cameron to his party mates was the following: "There's one thing Gordon Brown [the incumbent prime minister at the time] fears more than anything else: a Conservative Party that has the courage to change. So let's give him the fight of his life."[43]

ENGAGE IN NEW, UNTRADITIONAL ALLIANCES

"You can't win a presidential election alone." The son of a presidential candidate once told me that after they lost, and I agree one hundred percent. You need allies and alliances. The appeal of the top candidate and his willingness to reach out obviously play a key role in that respect. I think that alliances have become even more important today as politics is increasingly fragmented in many countries. As new parties rise out of nowhere and old parties weaken, you must be open to new, untraditional partnerships. Successful challengers also aggressively reach out to the business sector, key media outlets, religious groups, and civic groups. You should make a list of the main players and devote sufficient time to the outreach effort. Candidates should not be surprised about an initial resistance when doing this. In some cases, it will take several attempts, and you might have to first convince gatekeepers or trusted friends.

You should also chase key endorsements. One of the most impactful endorsements in modern election campaign history happened when Joe Biden ran for the Democratic nomination in 2020. At the time, Biden had performed poorly in the early states such as Iowa, New Hampshire, and Nevada, and his candidacy was in peril. The next state to vote was South Carolina, when Jim Clyburn, congressman from South Carolina and the highest ranking African American in Congress, endorsed Joe Biden. Biden had long been arguing that he had a tight relationship with the African American community in the state. The endorsement of Clyburn, one of the most influential political players in the state, added precious credibility to that claim. On election day in South Carolina, Biden won with 48.6 percent of the vote. It was a resounding victory that jump-started an important dynamic. An entire series of candidates and former rivals, such as Mayor Pete Buttigieg and Senator Amy Klobuchar, also endorsed Biden. All of a sudden, Biden was the one remaining moderate candidate in the primary race around whom the other moderates coalesced. The next round of voting took place a few days later on "Super Tuesday," when fourteen states held primaries. Biden won ten out of the fourteen, in many of which he did not run TV ads, and had no field offices. Biden went on to win the Democratic nomination, and Clyburn's endorsement was crucial to make it happen because it dramatically changed the dynamics of the race.

APPEAL TO PATRIOTISM

In French presidential elections, it is often said that France gives itself to the one who wants it the most. It's true for other countries as well, and I would like to add that a country usually gives itself to the one who *is* the country the most. I sometimes ask that question explicitly in my strategic surveys for clients: among the candidates, which one is the most typical Indonesian, Malaysian, or Brazilian? Oftentimes, the one who is seen as most typical for the country is also the one who is on top in the voting. This doesn't mean that it has to be the most nationalistic candidate. In their answers, voters sometimes refer to the looks of the candidate or his life story. The key for a candidate is to be the one who best connects with the attitudes toward life of a country's citizens at the time.

Especially progressive opposition candidates often mistakenly assume that conservatives have a monopoly on patriotism. You can argue for change and love your country at the same time. These are not mutually exclusive. The French left is a great example of that. When François Hollande ran to unseat incumbent Nicolas Sarkozy as president of France, he declared that France is not the problem, it's the solution.[44] At the beginning of the campaign, he gave a signature speech in which he said, "I came here to talk to you about France and the republic." He then continued, "Don't look for this election to be about partisan fights. This campaign goes beyond that, beyond the left. The stake of this election, three months before the first round, it's France. It's France always."*

What followed was a patriotic, rhetoric firework and an impressive electoral win. He became the first challenger in almost three decades to unseat an incumbent French president.

---

* "Je suis venu vous parler de la France, et donc de la République. [..] L'enjeu de cette campagne qui commence, n'allez pas le chercher dans un affrontement partisan. L'enjeu de cette campagne va bien au-delà de nous, de la Gauche. L'enjeu de cette campagne, à trois mois du premier tour, c'est la France. C'est la France, toujours." "L'intégralité du discours de François Hollande au Bourget," *L'Obs*, January 26, 2012, https://www.nouvelobs.com/election-presidentielle-2012/sources-brutes/20120122.OBS9488/l-integralite-du-discours-de-francois-hollande-au-bourget.html.

MOVE BEYOND TRADITIONAL LEFT AND RIGHT

When Bill Clinton ran for president, one of the challenges he was facing was that his party, the Democrats, was seen as too liberal. As a result, he positioned himself as a "new Democrat," more centrist than the national party leadership, and tried to move beyond the traditional dichotomy of left versus right. When he announced his candidacy, he said the following:

> The change we must make isn't liberal or conservative. It's both, and it's different. The small towns and main streets of America aren't like the corridors and backrooms of Washington. People out here don't care about the idle rhetoric of "left" and "right" and "liberal" and "conservative" and all the other words that have made our politics a substitute for action. These families are crying out desperately for someone who believes the promise of America is to help them with their struggle to get ahead, to offer them a green light instead of a pink slip.[45]

The same theme is also present in his acceptance speech at the Democratic National Convention:

> The choice we offer is not conservative or liberal; Democratic or Republican. It is different. It is new. And it will work. It will work because it is rooted in the vision and the values of the American people.[46]

In fact, at a certain point in his acceptance speech, he made change sound like a very traditional thing to do. Following his logic, voting for change would mean to go back to a situation that was present before but got lost along the way: "In the end, the New Covenant simply asks us all to be Americans again—old-fashioned Americans for a new time. Opportunity, responsibility, community."[47] It is quite a brilliant rhetorical move!

USE THE PERSONAL BACKGROUND AND LIFE STORY OF THE TOP CANDIDATE TO SHOW MAINSTREAM AND MIDDLE-CLASS LIFESTYLE AND VALUES

A key vulnerability of incumbents is that they are usually living a different life from most of their constituents. They are often detached from the daily lives of voters and risk looking out of touch. Challengers can exploit that by portraying a middle-class lifestyle and mainstream values. They should be seen in the media engaging with average voters. They should know everything about daily life, such as the price of milk, bread, gasoline, or a doctor's visit. In other words, they should show that they connect with average voters. The key here is to get closer to voters than the incumbents are. I have worked for a businessman who wanted to run for mayor in his city. Two and a half years before the election, we started our collaboration. He toured his city regularly, attended wakes, and provided livelihood trainings. By the time of the election, he was so established that he ran literally unopposed and went from private citizen to mayor.

ENDING EIGHTEEN YEARS OF OPPOSITION: THE BEST CASE STUDY ON HOW TO SELL CHANGE

The most comprehensive case study on how to make voters comfortable with voting for change is the British Labour Party. Some of you might remember how Tony Blair ended eighteen years of opposition, leading Labour to a landslide victory in 1997. After that, he went on to deliver two more national election wins for Labour. At the time of writing, no Labour prime minister in the UK before or after him has been able to achieve that. That fact alone makes it a tremendously interesting case study, but there is yet another reason. Because of various institutional factors (the absence of primaries, the party system, relatively high turnout), British elections are truly decided in the political center. Simplifying a bit, Labour and the Conservatives (or Tories, as they are sometimes called) compete for power, and the swing—meaning the number of people who switch between them—is of particular importance. As I mentioned at the beginning of the chapter, courting the center has become out of fashion in many countries, but looking at cases like the British Labour Party offers a way out of the gridlock, and it can be of great inspiration to opposition parties around the world. One of the people who was key in that effort was Philip Gould, a British political consultant. He worked extensively on the modernization of the Labour Party from 1984 until it won power in 1997, and beyond that point while Labour was governing. His book *The Unfinished Revolution: How New Labour Changed British Politics Forever*, which is his professional memoir, offers an inside look at the transformation of the Labour Party and is the basis for much of what I write in this section.[48]

By the time Tony Blair ran to become the leader of the party, Labour had been in the opposition for fifteen years and had lost three elections in a row. Sometimes, a governing party that loses reelection and is sent to the opposition benches has a good chance to win back some seats in the next election. Occasionally, this happens almost automatically once the new government has lost its first appeal. This had not been the case for the British Labour Party, which had run on a pointedly leftist platform. "Labour was more like a cult than a party," Tony Blair writes in his memoirs. "If you were to progress in it, you had to speak the language and press the right buttons."[49] Before Blair became the party leader, Labour did what many opposition parties first do, namely, to change their visual appearance and the look and feel of their materials. Throughout those years, Blair knew that that was not enough. The remake of the party had to be more substantive and include a repositioning of the party in the political center.[50] During the intraparty campaign for the party leadership, Blair had laid out many of the themes that would become central to his discourse. He advocated "change and renewal," "traditional principles but modern application," and "honoring the past but not living in it."[51] At the age of forty-one, Blair looked like the leader of a modern party. Right after his designation as party leader, Labour jumped about ten points in the surveys. Blair and his team knew full well, though, that the effect might evaporate. Labour had led in the surveys leading up to previous elections, only to lose on election day.

In his memoirs, Blair reflects on the fact that he had a different purpose for the renewal effort than did his predecessors as party leaders. He writes that the latter presented renewal to the party as something they had to do in order to compromise with the electorate and come into power. For Blair, on the other hand, the modernization was something he wanted to do. "It may sound a subtle difference, but it is fundamental," he writes.[52] I absolutely agree because it makes the entire effort much more believable. In that respect, I have often noticed that partisans on both sides of the political spectrum see centrism as wishy-washy or even as a betrayal. By doing so, they fail to understand that one can feel equally strongly and passionately about a centrist position as they feel about theirs.

At the first party conference after being elected as the party leader, Blair gave a passionate speech. In this address, he clearly told the party in which direction he intended to lead: "Colleagues, the people of this country are not looking to us for a revolution," he said. He then continued:

> Some of you will think we are too modest in our aims, too cautious. Some of you, I hear, support me simply because you think I can win. (Laughter) Actually, that is not a bad reason for

> supporting me, but it is not enough. I want more. We are not going to win despite our beliefs. We will only win because of our beliefs. (Applause) I want to win not because the Tories are despised, but because we are understood, supported, trusted. And there is no choice between being principled and unelectable and electable and unprincipled. We have tortured ourselves with this foolishness for too long.[53]

Blair is a formidable public speaker. As he went on, he made the case for the Labour Party to modernize:

> I want to tell you something. At the next election the voters will have had this Tory government for 17 or 18 years. They may hate them, but they know them. I want them now to know us, our identity, our character as a party, and change is an important part of that. We have changed. We were right to change. Parties that do not change die, and this party is a living movement not an historical monument. (Applause) If the world changes and we do not, we become of no use to the world. Our principles cease being principles and just ossify. We have not changed to forget our principles, but to fulfill them, not to lose our identity but to keep our relevance. Change is an important part of gaining the nation's trust.[54]

Blair also started to consistently use the term "New Labour," which de facto renamed the party. Some people ridiculed this by adding "New Labour, New Underwear." They were implying that it was merely a slogan, empty of content and lacking substance, but I think this is a dramatic underestimation of the profundity of the strategic process that took place.

Effective campaigns are as much about listening as they are about speaking. Blair says that any attempt to win power for an opposition party should start with an honest assessment of why the party is in the opposition. In his assessment, the British Labour Party had wasted a lot of time in the opposition escaping the true reason for defeat.[55] The key cause was a disconnect between Labour's political offer and its natural target audience, the middle class, which had become more diversified and more upwardly mobile. The modernization of the party therefore also meant that New Labour would not try to sell something to get the votes of people but was really trying to reconnect and understand the middle class.

Blair's team therefore started to conduct regular focus groups with voters that had voted for the Conservative Party before but considered switching to Labour at the next election. One of the key findings was that swing voters not only disagreed with key Labour policies but were deeply afraid of them. Respondents feared that Labour would raise taxes, lacked fiscal control, and would enact policies that would ultimately result in inflation. More broadly, the focus groups also revealed that voters did not perceive Labour as addressing the issues that mattered to their daily lives. Instead, they thought of Labour as a party that was ideologically driven, talking about issues that only mattered to a minority of voters. This is an important takeaway: a party that wants to represent ordinary people talks about things that matter to ordinary people, not about ideology. I know this sounds simple, yet progressive parties in particular fail to act on that in many cases. Blair also says, and I agree, that the left is rarely rejected because of its values. Social justice, fairness, equality, and community are indeed values that many people share in principle. It is almost always the specific policies the left proposes to realize these values that get them in trouble with the public.[56] Thus, it became clear based on the findings from the focus groups that Labour had to abandon and change some key policy positions. From then on, modernization efforts could not only be limited to image, appearance, and rhetoric but had to include policies as well.

A key event in that respect would become the fight about the so-called Clause IV of the party constitution. Clause IV explains the aims and basic values of the party. It had been adopted in 1918 and was seen as the party's commitment to socialism. In particular, it called for the "common ownership of the means of production."[57] This was largely symbolic because, as Blair writes in his memoirs, few people except the far left really believed it even back then. Yet, no one had dared to remove it, and that was why Blair wanted to take it head-on. He writes:

> What this symbolized, therefore, was not just something redundant in our constitution, but a refusal to confront reality, to change profoundly, to embrace the modern world wholeheartedly. In other words, this symbol mattered.[58]

Blair therefore proposed a new clause, which stated Labour's belief that "by the strength of our common endeavor we achieve more than we achieve alone." The proposal further said that Labour wanted to create a "community in which power, wealth and opportunity are in the hands of the many, not the few, where the rights we enjoy reflect the duties we owe."[59] A special party conference was set to decide on the new clause. The battle was a key test for Blair. If he lost that internal vote, it would undermine his entire effort and promise of Labour's renewal. The gamble paid off and the new Clause IV was approved with 65 percent of the vote.[60] The process of the party leader fighting for the new clause and winning that battle was important for voters to witness. It signaled that not only was there a new head but that the party was willing to follow him along his course.

Another key battle was about taxes and about which party was credible in the voters' eyes on the issue. As mentioned earlier, higher taxes were one of the things that voters feared about Labour, and it is one of the issues that the Conservatives had used in the past to campaign against Labour. Taxes are also an issue that is directly felt by many voters, and it therefore became clear that Labour could probably not win power without neutralizing this weakness. An important figure to give New Labour fiscal and economic credibility was Gordon Brown, who later became the chancellor of the exchequer, the equivalent of the finance minister in other countries, and ultimately Blair's successor as prime minister. In later years, the relationship between Blair and Brown would become complex, but that is not the topic here. With respect to the creation of New Labour, the two were partners, and Brown announced that Labour would not increase the basic or the top tax rate. This was a crucial promise because it was simple, understandable, and easy for voters to track. In previous campaigns, Labour had tried to argue that it wanted to raise taxes only for the rich but lower taxes for most other people. It had turned out to be a difficult point to get across. The genie was out of the bottle, and Labour was put on the defense. It was a painful lesson for Labour, but the learning and the strategic adjustments based on it paid off. In his regular focus groups, Gould noticed that slowly, the Tories became seen as the party of the rich. And after some time, Labour started to lead the Tories in internal surveys on who could be trusted on taxes. This was a tremendous accomplishment for Labour and a crucial prerequisite to ultimately win back power.

Blair and the Labour team also realized that relying on the weakness of the incumbent Tories was not enough. This time around, there had to be more in store that would make it worthwhile to go out and vote for Labour. Labour came up with specific policy pledges that would be smaller promises than in the past but concrete and therefore hopefully more believable. This is an important point because Labour had always promised better schools and better hospitals before, but voters did not buy into the promise. They thought that Labour could not deliver, or that paying for it would be painful. These pledges were something that again was carefully tested in focus groups. Gould found out that if Labour would say how it planned to pay for each pledge, this would make the pledge even more believable. At the end of a long process of brainstorming and testing, Labour created a small card with a picture of Tony Blair on the front, and then on the back, the pledges were listed: cut class size to thirty students, fast-track punishment for persistent young offenders, cut National Health Service waiting lists by treating an extra one hundred thousand patients, get two hundred fifty thousand under-twenty-five-year-olds off benefits and into work, and no rise in income tax rates. On top of the card, it said "Keep this card and see that we keep our promises." At the bottom, it was signed by Tony Blair. According to Gould, the card with the pledges tested extraordinarily well when it was resubmitted to focus group respondents. "The pledges worked better than anything else I have tested in politics. Nothing else came close," he writes.[61]

Blair's plan for the final stretch of the campaign was to reassure voters. A key endorsement played an important role in that respect. Six weeks before the election, the *Sun*, the tabloid with the biggest circulation, declared its support for Tony Blair. This was tremendously important because in the UK, the press plays an openly political role, and the same newspaper had brutally attacked Blair's predecessors. This time, it declared on its front page that the Tories were tired and divided and that Blair had everything it took to take the country into the new millennium.[62]

On election day, New Labour won 43 percent of the vote and added 146 seats in Parliament.[63] An estimated 1.8 million former Conservative voters switched to Labour, the very essence of the New Labour strategy.[64] In his victory speech, Blair immediately continued the strategy of reassuring voters by declaring, "We have been elected as New Labour, and we will govern as New Labour."[65]

A THREE-TIME LOSER BECOMES THE MOST POPULAR POLITICIAN ON EARTH

Another fascinating case study of selling change to voters is the president of Brazil, Luiz Inácio Lula da Silva—Lula for short. In 2022, Lula won a comeback as president of Brazil after having spent more than a year in jail. While this is without any doubt a stunning political accomplishment, I cover an earlier stage of Lula's career in this chapter, which is no less fascinating. Lula ran for president of Brazil three times and lost three times. After that, he decided to run one more time but to do things differently than he had in the past. The changes he made in his approach to the campaign, including a personal makeover, became the cornerstone for a winning streak: he ran a fourth time and won, won reelection, arguably delivered victory to his successor, and then launched a comeback himself. How did he, a former union leader without much formal education, accomplish that? A lot of what I write in this chapter in order to answer that question is based on conversations with Brazilian political consultants I interviewed in Brazil as part of the research I carried out for my PhD.[66]

When Brazil was still ruled by the military, Lula helped found the Brazilian Worker's Party, the *Partido dos Trabalhadores* (PT). It brought together a colorful mix of unionists, workers, intellectuals, Catholics, Leninists, and Marxists. The two journalists, Sue Branford and Bernardo Kucinski, wrote that the PT became one of the few mass parties in Latin America that understood itself as more than an electoral platform.[67] It had a clearly leftist program with the goal of a radical change of society. In that sense, the PT back then understood elections as a means to achieve its ultimate goal, a socialist society. Later on, Lula became one of the most prominent faces of the PT, and after the military regime had ended, Lula also stood as the PT candidate in the election for governor of São Paulo. Lula campaigned as "a Brazilian just like you" and lost badly. It turned out that the majority of voters did not want a governor like themselves.[68] The episode illustrated a problem that would haunt Lula for many elections to come: as in other developing countries, the poor in Brazil do not automatically vote for a candidate from the poor. As for middle-class voters, they were deeply skeptical of a candidate such as Lula.

In 1989, Brazilians elected their president in a direct election for the first time in nearly three decades. The PT nominated Lula as its presidential candidate, and he campaigned on a classic leftist platform. He proposed to nationalize the entire banking sector and told an audience in the US that he would consider defaulting on Brazil's foreign debt.[69] Another hot issue was land—a topic I've helped address in several developing countries myself. In sympathy with the landless movement occupying land across Brazil, Lula also campaigned for land reform. During the course of the campaign, Lula became the target of brutal attacks. Many of these attacks would be repeated in future campaigns and implied that the election of Lula would pose a serious threat to the Brazilian economy. For example, according to Wendy Hunter, the president of one of the country's main business federations, the Federation of Industries of the State of São Paulo (FIESP), claimed that, in the case of a Lula victory, eight hundred thousand businessmen would leave Brazil.[70] After an intense campaign, and despite the many accusations, Lula placed second on election day with 17 percent of the vote.[71]

Similar to Argentina and France, Brazil has a so-called runoff system with two rounds of voting. The two candidates who get the most votes in the first round then face each other in a runoff. Since Lula made it to rank two (edging out his competition from the left), he qualified. In the second round of voting, he was able to considerably improve his vote share to 47 percent.[72] Hunter explains that while Lula had lost the election, the result was nevertheless seen as a relative success and felt like a victory for the PT. The problem with that was that the party also handled the result as a victory internally, meaning that it primarily looked at outside factors as an explanation for why Lula did not create the ultimate surprise by winning the election. It blamed the loss on the bias of the media, the poorly educated electorate, the prejudice against a manual worker with limited official education, and the abuse of the financial advantage of the opponent.[73] Admittedly, these were probably all factors that did have an impact on the result, but this reasoning also kept the party leadership from looking at internal factors that they could affect.

A consequence of this was that Lula and the PT would basically rerun the same campaign again in future elections. Brazilian society evolved in the meantime, however. During the 1990s, inflation became a major issue. Fernando Henrique Cardoso, the minister of finance at the time, implemented the so-called *Plano Real* (Real Plan), which was aimed at stabilizing the Brazilian currency, the real, and bringing inflation in Brazil under control. At first, the PT dismissed it as an elite and bourgeois concern, which was a big mistake. Inflation is an issue that hits absolutely everyone, including and foremost the poorest segments of the population. It may not be existential for every voter, but all voters are impacted by it. In that sense, the PT was also caught off guard by the relative success of the *Plano Real*. Cardoso's claim that a strong currency would lead to higher wages and more purchasing power became increasingly credible and had strong appeal for many Brazilians.[74] The success of the plan was a key factor in why Cardoso won the presidential election outright without a runoff two times in a row. Lula, on the other hand, lost brutally, twice ranking a distant number two.

The election results also underlined a fundamental problem for Lula. Simply put, the Brazilian electorate was split into three groups. There was one-third of the electorate that would always vote for Lula no matter what he said, did, or promised during the campaign. Since he did have a committed, loyal base, he would also fare well in surveys that were taken a long time before the election, when other potential opponents were not known yet. Another third of the electorate would never vote for Lula, no matter what he would say, do, or promise. Finally, one-third of the electorate was up for grabs. They had serious reservations and doubts about Lula but had not closed the door on voting for him. During his first three campaigns, Lula and the PT always geared their campaign toward the first third of the electorate, the loyal base, and ended up losing on election day.

Maybe you wonder why it took Lula three consecutive losses over a period of thirteen years to figure out that his base is not enough to win. It's actually a common, and I think natural, tendency for politicians to want to please party staff, members, and activists with their campaigns. However, unless a pure mobilization strategy is enough to win, the party base is rarely the only main target of a campaign. While this seems obvious to me, I have witnessed such behavior so often that I have given it some thought. Over the years, I concluded that it has a lot to do with many politicians looking for instant gratification.

Going back to Lula, one can only imagine that after having lost three consecutive presidential elections, he must have had moments of frustration. When he launched a fourth attempt, he made it clear to the party that he wanted key things in the campaign to change. This is an important point because the PT was organized rather tightly and Lula had less independence when it came to deciding on his campaign message and strategy than, for example, a presidential candidate in the United States. When preparing for his fourth attempt, Lula insisted on working together with a famous Brazilian political consultant, the late José Eduardo Mendoça or Duda Mendoça, as he was often called. Mendoça had run many successful election campaigns, both at home in Brazil and internationally. I personally met and interviewed him when I conducted research for my PhD. Mendoça told me that he started his work for Lula by carrying out a comprehensive round of public opinion research, namely focus group discussions. He wanted to find out what had gone wrong in the past.[75] For Lula and his party, this was an important paradigm shift on how they approached the campaign. From now on, the campaign would not be geared toward the base but would be oriented toward the third of the electorate in the middle.

To begin with, that third was a heterogeneous group. In terms of socioeconomic characteristics, it consisted of voters with the lowest level of education and income, but it also included parts of the middle class, female voters, and the elderly.[76] Similar to the British Labour Party that I discussed earlier, the focus groups also revealed that some Brazilian voters not only had disagreed with Lula's policies in the past but were really afraid of them. As mentioned, Lula's opponents had always successfully played up that fear. As a result, it was clear to Lula and Mendoça that it would take a continued and strategic effort to make voters comfortable with the prospect of a Lula presidency.

Mendoça says, and I absolutely agree, that two things matter in an election campaign: form and substance. What he means by this is that it is not one or the other; they are both equally important and in effect go hand in hand.[77] With respect to substance, the key change was that Lula would embrace the monetary policy of the incumbent president, Fernando Henrique Cardoso. This was a significant change since Lula had vigorously opposed it only four years ago. Lula released a letter to the Brazilian people, the *Carta ao povo brasileiro,* in which he pledged that his government would respect all national and international contracts.[78] By that time, monetary stability was nothing new for voters and it was obvious that the *Plano Real* had been at least moderately successful. Agreeing to the monetary policy allowed Lula to focus on other issues, such as social and employment matters. In other words, Lula no longer offered a radical change of society but rather different priorities for Brazil. Ted G. Goertzel, a professor at Rutgers University in New Jersey, observes an interesting point: while Lula's rhetoric of change was certainly still emotional, it had become rather vague on the specifics. On the other hand, he was very precise in his promises about what would *not* change in a Lula presidency. He promised that his government would do the following:

- honor all international commitments made by its predecessor;
- control inflation;
- maintain a floating exchange rate; and
- maintain a budgetary surplus before payments on debts.[79]

I think that the above specifics are important here because it makes the promise of embracing the monetary policy of his predecessor more credible.

Another key aspect of Lula's new strategy was alliances with other parties. Brazil has an extremely fragmented party system, and for his fourth run for the presidency, Lula wanted the party to be more open with respect to alliances with other parties. Brazil is also a federalist system in which the states have considerable power, and the governors are often called the fourth branch of government. Lula and his inner circle therefore thought that it was essential to get the support of key governors, even if they did not belong to the left.[80] Part of the new alliance strategy was also the choice of Lula's vice presidential candidate. As in the US, the vice president of Brazil is elected on the same ticket as the president. Lula selected José Alencar, who was a member of the center-right Liberal Party and one of the richest businessmen in the country. It was a stark contrast to the previous election, when Lula chose a known leftist, Leonel Brizola, as his running mate. The selection of Alencar was an important signal to the business community—especially in São Paulo, the economic center of the country—that they would have a direct ally in a Lula government. It showed that Lula had an open ear for the business community, which led to important trust and even some limited support among the community. Some observers went as far as to say that thanks to this outreach, the rich elite of the country allowed Lula's election to happen. On top of that, there was another benefit to the selection: Alencar opened up a link to the evangelical churches, which are another factor in Brazilian elections. The Liberal Party was known to have strong ties with the evangelical movement, and Alencar himself belonged to an evangelical church.

While the substance obviously changed, the form of Lula's campaign also changed considerably. In previous attempts, Lula would look like a combative, angry, sweating union leader. The focus groups revealed that female voters in particular were turned off by it. In his fourth run, he looked and acted like a statesman and dressed in more formal clothes. He wore elegant suits with a perfectly knotted tie. His team would provide him with identical shirts that he could change throughout the day so that the sweating would be less noticeable. In his campaign commercials, Lula was often surrounded by well-educated and respected experts from numerous fields. Lula campaigned with the slogan *paz e amor* (peace and love). The tagline clearly did not communicate a revolution. "Do not worry, everything will be fine with Lula," was basically the message. In a survey shortly before the election, Lula was ahead of his opponents on who would do most for the poor, who would create jobs, and who would have the best plan for government. He was also ahead on who would be the most honest and trustworthy.[81] Cleary, the effort of policy moderation and reassuring voters had paid off and this was the raw material out of which a victory could happen. On election day for the first round, Lula was clearly ahead, distancing his closest rival by more than twenty percentage points. He went on to win the presidency in the second round with 61 percent of the vote.

When I conducted the interviews about Lula with Brazilian political consultants, two questions were constantly on my mind. First, why did voters believe Lula's moderation strategy? After all, he had been around for a long time and was not exactly a new player on the national stage. His image was well defined over the time period of more than a decade. Second, why did the party go along with the approach? Regarding the latter question, the evolution of the PT into a government party was indeed a long and difficult process. The party consisted of several factions, with Lula belonging to the dominant and less radical one. But each step toward modernization and policy moderation was the result of long discussions and negotiations. During the process, Lula used his clout with the party, and the party had few alternatives to Lula. He was the face of the party, and clearly someone who could appeal to voters beyond party lines. In addition to that, Lula also circumvented the party. He founded and used the Citizenship Institute, *Instituto da Cidadania Brasil,* to engage in a dialogue with stakeholders beyond the PT. The institute organized roundtables with governors and business leaders and allowed Lula access to the business community without his party.[82] This was done years before the election and was an important preparation for the actual campaign. In that sense, the choice of Alencar as running mate did not come out of nowhere. It can clearly be seen as the culmination of this outreach effort. With respect to his letter to the public that I mentioned above, the more radical wing of the party was not pleased with it. There was little that they could do, though, since it did not come from the party but was a letter written by Lula as a person. The approach allowed Lula to be his own messenger with a certain distance from the party ideology.

With respect to the credibility of Lula's moderation effort in the voter's eyes, the Brazilian political consultants I interviewed saw several reasons for it. Up until then, PT politicians were seen as comparatively clean. While the PT was seen as dogmatic, and there was infighting, PT members in the House of Representatives were rarely accused of corruption up until that time. While other *deputados* would switch parties often or were accused of engaging in shady deals to get pork barrel spending, few PT deputies faced such allegations. In addition, Cardoso and his party had moved to the right of the political spectrum over the years. This opened up space in the center-left of Brazil's party system that the PT could fill.[83] Over the years, the PT had also won several local offices. Not all of these experiences were equally successful and the coordination with the goals of the national party would sometimes be a challenge, but overall, the PT in government was seen as honest, caring, and innovative. Projects such as the *Bolsa Escola,* a stipend underprivileged families received if they sent their children to school, were first created on the local level and would later become nationwide projects. The local officials of the PT also made citizen participation and transparency key elements of their administrations. Ghost employees were fired and the bidding for local contracts became more open.[84] This concrete governing responsibility at the local level also became a driver for more pragmatism within the party. Indeed, a mayor has to solve specific problems and address the daily concerns of his citizens, while a member of parliament—especially as part of the opposition—can simply criticize the national government. Similar to the president, a mayor also has to win a runoff in the Brazilian system and therefore needs to get a majority of the votes. Two years before the presidential elections, Brazil held local elections. In terms of preparations, this round of municipal elections played a crucial and strategic role for the preparation of the presidential elections. Even if they were local elections, the party approached them with a nationwide strategy and a coherent message.[85] While Lula was not on the ballot himself, he toured the country and was the national face of the campaign. As a result of this effort, the PT was able to get mayors elected in a number of major cities, which was an important preparation for the ground game of Lula's fourth and ultimately successful run for the presidency. From the time when democracy was reintroduced in Brazil, the PT was also the only major party that had never been in government at the national level. By the time Lula ran for the fourth time he was the natural alternative to the status quo, and many gave him the benefit of the doubt. In the end, people believe what they want to believe, and many voters found Lula's offer appealing and wanted to believe that he would improve their lives.

As a conclusion of this chapter, let me repeat my preferred tactics to make voters comfortable with voting for change:

- Showcase moderate and successful government record at the local level.
- Neutralize a historic weakness on a specific issue (for example, taxes or the environment).
- Use a key issue or statement to show ideological distance from your own party.
- Engage in new and untraditional alliances.
- Secure endorsement from key politicians.
- Appeal to patriotism.
- Move beyond traditional left and right policies.
- Use the personal background and life story of the top candidate to show mainstream and middle-class values.
- Change the look and feel of the party.
- Nominate a top candidate who looks like change.
- Reach out to key media outlets, religious groups and the business sector.
- Agree with and adopt key aspects of the incumbent's platform.
- Nominate a moderate vice presidential candidate.
- Surround yourself with respected experts.

LAST PIECE OF ADVICE

I mentioned in this chapter that a challenger should seek key endorsements and that sometimes, this requires several attempts. This said, what do you do if a key player you are chasing really does not want to endorse you (yet)? You endorse the politician in question. You mention this person as your role model, as the reason why you entered politics, or what role he would play in your administration. "If elected, I would choose the former president as special envoy to the Middle East" or "I would put him in charge as the border czar," just to give two examples.

5

MAXIMIZE THE ADVANTAGES OF THE CHALLENGER

A candidate's biggest strength is often also the biggest weakness. As I mentioned in chapter 1, incumbents enjoy significant advantages over challengers in terms of awareness, legitimacy to hold the office, absence of intraparty competition, and fundraising capabilities. This being said, incumbency also comes with unique vulnerabilities, namely a government record to defend. If voters are unhappy with how things are going in the country, state, or city, incumbents get the blame almost automatically. The distinct advantage of challengers is that they are free to criticize and attack the records of the incumbents. Challengers also often benefit from the fact that they are the new kid in town and therefore become an object of interest to the media. As they advocate change, their campaigns can benefit from tremendous energy and turn into real grassroots movements. In this chapter, I share my expertise on how you can take maximum advantage of these distinct challenger opportunities. In recent times, there have been several successful candidates that were outsiders to politics, and who were particularly skillful in that respect. I'm thinking, for example, of Ukrainian president Volodymyr Zelensky and French president Emmanuel Macron. In both cases, the presidency was the first political office they had run for, and both won in a landslide. They accomplished that by taking challenger tactics to a new level and therefore serve as a great inspiration to other candidates. In the second part of the chapter, on the contrary, I explain what traps a challenger should avoid and how to neutralize any weakness.

DOUBLE DOWN ON BEING AN OUTSIDER

Before running for president of Ukraine, Volodymyr Zelensky was a famous and successful actor, comedian, and head of his own production company. After Russia's attack on Ukraine in February 2022, Zelensky soon became famous around the world for his active style of crisis communication. He addressed various parliaments, gave media interviews, and relentlessly released videos on social media, but that is a topic for another book. At this point, I am interested in how he, a political novice, got himself elected as president of Ukraine in 2019, defeating incumbent president Petro Poroshenko.

I have visited Ukraine repeatedly, have spoken to numerous local politicians and political operatives, and even had the opportunity to watch some focus groups. Poroshenko, one of the richest businessmen in the country, came to power after the so-called Maidan Revolution, a popular uprising during the winter 2013–14. He was elected outright in the first round of voting. By the time he ran for reelection five years later, Ukrainian voters had become extremely unhappy with the status quo. A majority disapproved of the job the incumbent president was doing and thought that the country was headed in the wrong direction. Various surveys showed Poroshenko garnering between 10 percent and 20 percent of the vote. Voters were not only dissatisfied with the status quo but angry with the incumbent president and the entire political class. This was the opening for Zelensky, who, as mentioned earlier, was well known as a comedian but lacked any kind of political experience whatsoever. Steven Derix and Marina Shelkunova are two journalists who wrote an interesting biography about Zelensky. They write that, among other things, Zelensky had played the main character in a TV show called *Servant of the People*. Vasyl Holoborodko, the protagonist, was a schoolteacher who became president of Ukraine unexpectedly and by ranting about omnipresent corruption in Ukraine.[86] In many ways, Zelensky's election campaign was more a continuation of that TV show than a traditional campaign. Unlike the other candidates, Zelensky did not tour the country or hold press conferences, nor did he give speeches. As a matter of fact, he spent much of the campaign period shooting the next season of the TV show.[87]

Be that as it may, it doesn't mean that Zelensky's campaign was a spontaneous act. Serhii Rudenko, a Ukrainian journalist and political commentator, writes that Zelensky had planned the campaign launch for many months prior to declaring.[88] Among other things, he learned Ukrainian and registered a party with the same name as his TV show, Servant of the People. The campaign itself came across as informal and certainly with much less pathos than usual in Ukrainian politics, but it was carefully staged. Zelensky's core message was that Ukraine needed honest politicians if it ever wanted to get rid of corruption. When Zelensky declared his candidacy on New Year's Eve 2018, a few minutes before midnight, he spoke about three possible paths for Ukrainians to choose: live as before, go abroad, or try to change things.[89]

His claim was credible in part also because he himself was seen as not corruptible. As a comedian, he has always made fun of politicians from all political sides, including the most powerful ones. Since he had never taken sides politically, including during the Maidan Revolution, he appealed to all parts of the electorate.

What's of particular interest for other challengers is how Zelensky dealt with his political inexperience. Instead of trying to make up for it, he doubled down on it and took maximum advantage of the situation. In that sense, Zelensky did not even try to come up with a political program but told voters that they could send in ideas and proposals. Many did.[90] He avoided taking positions on issues such as joining the European Union or NATO by promising to hold a referendum on those questions should he be elected. With millions of followers, social media became a key tool to build the movement of his de facto campaign. This approach also allowed the candidate to avoid most press scrutiny, as Zelensky only did some softball media appearances.

Ukraine also has a system with a runoff for presidential elections. Zelensky easily qualified for the second round, in which he faced off against incumbent Poroshenko. Between the first and second round of voting, there was a public debate. Zelensky spent days preparing for the showdown.[91] While he was not accustomed to giving political statements, he absolutely was a skilled performer. During the face-off between the two candidates, Zelensky literally prosecuted Poroshenko. "How can it be that Ukraine is one of the poorest countries in Europe, when it is governed by the richest President in history?" he asked.[92] He also told incumbent President Poroshenko, "I am not your opponent. I am your verdict."[93] Bingo! I said earlier that an election with an incumbent is foremost a referendum on the incumbent, and the verdict statement brilliantly sums up that approach to a challenger campaign. The debate sealed the deal for many voters, and Zelensky was elected president of Ukraine with 73 percent of the vote.

A key prerequisite for Zelensky's success was that the electorate was deeply frustrated not only with the status quo and the incumbent but with the entire political class. By voting for Zelensky, voters wanted to get rid of the whole political personnel. This sentiment that the political system is rotten, and all politicians are corrupt, was the raw material from which Zelensky could create his stunning upset. The day Zelensky was inaugurated as president, he doubled down on his approach by dissolving parliament. The move paid off: in the subsequent parliamentary election, Zelensky's newly founded party, Servant of the People, crushed all established parties and won an outright majority in parliament.

After the election, Zelensky's bid was sometimes described as the first solely social media campaign. While the campaign certainly used social media effectively, I think that this is nevertheless a misreading of history. Having been a known figure and appearing weekly on one of the most popular TV channels in the country each week—playing the president—was tremendously important for his campaign. Zelensky had also toured the entire country as an actor for many years, and while doing that he was featured in local media as well. By the time he became a politician, he knew his country, people, and media environment extremely well.

There is another important lesson that Zelensky's case teaches us. Pundits and journalists will always ask any challenger to get specific with his proposals. It is possible to do that in a disciplined, limited, and well-tested manner, as the example of Tony Blair's Labour Party and the card with the pledges showed. Making specific proposals is nonetheless a risky undertaking because it makes you vulnerable to attacks. Voters in focus groups will always say that they want to hear specifics, and—generally speaking—it does sound great. Who doesn't want to hear specifics? No focus group respondent will ever say "you know what, I prefer to keep things really vague." This, nonetheless, does not mean that voters will like *your* specifics. My advice is to not fall into the trap. As mentioned, it is key to show contrast with your opponent on the main issue, and I recommend having a select number of concrete proposals that you are sure resonate with your target audience. Wading into unnecessary details is, however, ill advised. I think that asking for specifics is often an excuse for voters who cannot make up their minds. During the 2020 US presidential election campaign, for example, it became common that live focus groups on various TV channels would discuss the presidential and vice presidential debates. They particularly zoomed in on undecided voters from swing states who could potentially influence the outcome of the election. After having seen Donald Trump in office for four years, and after four hours of debates, many of these focus group respondents were still undecided and were asking for more specifics. Chances are they remained undecided.

THE OLD PARTY SYSTEM COLLAPSES AND THE NEW KID IN TOWN BENEFITS

This next example comes from the 2017 presidential election in France. By the time the country approached the election season, incumbent president François Hollande from the Socialist Party had become so unpopular that something rare happened—Hollande decided he wouldn't even try and run for reelection. This illustrates to what extent the electorate was looking for change. One of the ministers serving in Hollande's cabinet did think about running, though—Emmanuel Macron. Unknown to the broader public only a few years earlier, Macron entered the race and, as we now know, ended up being elected (and reelected) president of France. At the young age of thirty-nine years, and without having run for elected office before, he won the presidency with a stunning 66.1 percent of the vote.[94]

Here's the story: Macron was a private citizen and investment banker before becoming first an adviser of economic affairs to President Hollande and later his minister for economic affairs. You might wonder, how was Macron able to credibly represent change if he was associated with the unpopular incumbent government? The key was that Macron not only offered a message of change but decided to literally run against the entire political system. He stepped down as minister, left the government and the Socialist Party, and founded a new party. To be precise, he first founded a movement, named On the Move, *en Marche!* (EM), which was only later transformed into a party. The initials of the movement were, nonetheless, a hint that supporting Macron as a presidential candidate was the main purpose of the effort. In that sense, members were closer to fans or groupies than to traditional party activists. Signing up was free and easy to do online, and as a result, the movement soon had more members than traditional parties.[95] Local events were organized, and Macron started to tour the country to give speeches, which attracted big crowds across France. In addition, a tremendous grassroots effort was launched. Its purpose was to listen to voters that had never been engaged in politics before and to make a detailed diagnosis of the state of France. Volunteers knocked on three hundred thousand doors, held one hundred thousand conversations with voters, and filled out twenty-five hundred questionnaires.[96] This all served as a basis for Macron's political offer to come.

I speak French fluently, so I have had the opportunity to listen to the original Macron speeches. When he officially announced his candidacy, he offered lots of classic challenger rhetoric.[97] The speech is also remarkably patriotic, populist, and targeted against the entire political system. He said roughly that he was in politics for a short period of time but long enough to see what is wrong. And what is wrong has little to do with the voters or the country itself (both are actually great) but with the political system. With that approach and discourse, Macron captured and embodied the spirit of the French constitution very well. As an exchange student many years ago, I took classes in constitutional law at the Faculty of Law in Aix-en-Provence in Southern France. One of the things I learned was that when the direct election of the president by the people was introduced in France, it was a way to circumvent the political class and take a case directly to the people. That's exactly what Macron did.

His message was only credible because he had stepped down as minister and had founded his own party. Looking back, I think that if the exact same Macron had decided to compete for the official nomination of the governing Socialist Party, he would not have made it to the Elysée Palace. He would have had a hard time winning the nomination, and if he did, he would have been unable to make such a fundamental and compelling call for change of the political system. It is much more likely that the weight of the unpopular incumbent government would have tanked him. An important point in that respect is that when Macron stepped down as minister and announced his candidacy for president, incumbent president Hollande had not yet announced whether or not he would seek reelection. In other words, Macron took the risk of potentially running against his mentor and former boss. For a moment, at least, it must have felt like treason for Hollande that Macron, whom he appointed to the government, did not wait for his announcement. For Macron, however, sacrificing his former boss was key in distancing himself from the Hollande government. It made it clear to everyone that he was not the chosen successor of Hollande, nor would he defend his record.

It is also important to note that from an ideological point of view, Macron was placed in the political center. With respect to policy, Macron did not offer a revolution but centrism. Having served in the government of the Socialist president, he was considered by the right to be a leftist. Given his former professional background as an investment banker, the left never saw him as truly one of their own. To be precise, Macron left the Socialist Party through its right-hand door but stopped short of joining a party on the center-right. This made him potentially electable to many voters, but it was also a risk. Traditionally, the left and the right were the main political camps in France, and having positioned himself in the center, Macron started without a large base.

The gamble paid off for Macron due to several factors falling into place. To begin with, the French Socialist Party had never modernized itself. Its look and feel as well as the party discourse were traditionally leftist. To make matters worse, the party nominated a candidate who was associated with the radical wing of the party and whose positioning was out of step with many voters. On the right, the main candidate faced a major scandal involving family members as ghost employees in his office. He never recovered from the blow and was later sentenced to jail. As for the political center, major players decided not to run. In other words, the old political system literally fell apart, and by that time, Macron had perfectly positioned himself to benefit from it.

The case of Macron illustrates yet another crucial point, which is challengers are often new faces for the media, which means new stories to tell. While this can also be a liability, which I discuss in the chapter on crisis communication, it's mostly an opportunity. The media and the public alike will be interested to learn more about the challenger's background—where they come from, how they were brought up, their family, and other parts of the story they have to tell. If you think about it the other way around, no journalist will care how the sitting president was brought up or about the childhood of the incumbent prime minister unless it is related to a scandal. With respect to their daily reporting, the media will challenge the incumbent with everything that goes wrong, from the budget deficit, to failed reform plans, to a health crisis.

In the case of Emmanuel Marcon, he was an outsider in a political system that traditionally had not been particularly open to outsiders. French politicians often attended the same dedicated schools—the so-called *grandes écoles*—that prepared them for a political career. Those careers often lasted exceedingly long, with the same names being around for decades. By itself, the fact that a young investment banker became minister, under a Socialist president, made Macron already an object of interest to the media. He skillfully doubled down on his outsider status. In an interview, he declared, "If learning the job of a politician means to no longer tell the truth, lower your ambitions, enroll in role plays and appearances, then I will try every day not to learn the job of a politician."* From a journalist's point of view, Macron's story gets even better: his wife, Brigitte Trogneux, was his former teacher and is almost twenty-five years older than he. This was clearly different from any other previous politician's private life, which made it a tremendous media blockbuster. French professor Arnaud Benedetti writes that Macron indeed had tremendous appeal. When entering politics, Macron made the front page of countless entertainment magazines within months, repeatedly. Macron's look, his vacations, and his personal relationships were all of enormous interest to the media. He enjoyed a media presence that is out of reach for a traditional candidate.[98]

THE TRAP TO AVOID

Challengers have to make sure they are willing and able in view of their own record and ideological positioning to draw contrast with the incumbent on the dominant issue of the moment. In other words, if you don't go on the offense, you lose your biggest asset as a challenger. In sharp contrast to Zelensky and Macron, I now want to give you two examples of challengers who, for different reasons, were unable to put the incumbent on the defense. An instructive case on how challengers *should not run* is the German 2017 federal election. At that time, Martin Schulz of the Social Democratic Party, *Sozialdemokratische Partei Deutschlands* (SPD), tried to unseat incumbent chancellor Angela Merkel of the Christian Democratic Union, *Christlich Demokratische Union Deutschlands* (CDU). Prior to

---

* "Si 'apprendre le métier', c'est ne plus dire la vérité, c'est réduire ses ambitions, c'est s'inscrire dans un jeu de rôle ou d'apparences, alors je m'emploierai chaque jour à ne pas apprendre le métier politique." Emmanuel Macron on June 17, 2015, on BFM TV, quoted in François-Xavier Bourmaud, Emmanuel Macron: Les coulisses d'une victoire (Paris: Éditions de l'Archipel, 2017), 73.

that election, Merkel had governed together with the SPD in a so-called grand coalition. The term refers to the two big parties and traditional rivals for the chancellorship governing together in a national unity coalition. This was a problem for the SPD as the junior partner. If it wanted to overtake the CDU, it had to go on the offense, show contrast, and offer something different. Since the SPD was part of the same government as the CDU, much of their freedom to differentiate itself was taken away from the SPD.

To make an already difficult situation worse for the SPD, the dominant issue at the time was the refugee crisis. Two years before the general election, more than a million refugees had crossed the border into Germany. Chancellor Merkel famously said, "*wir schaffen das*" (we can do that), meaning that Germany can pull it off, absorb and integrate even such a big number of refugees.[99] It was a truly controversial and unpopular position, in particular for people on the right of the political spectrum. A new party, Alternative for Germany, *Alternative für Deutschland* (AfD), vigorously attacked Merkel and criticized her refugee policy. While Merkel thereby faced an increasingly vocal and strong challenge from the right, it was difficult for the SPD to take advantage of Merkel's vulnerability. Not only was the SPD part of the Merkel government, but it was also positioned on the center-left of the political spectrum. In that sense, while the SPD did not stand for open borders, it did advocate international solidarity and cooperation. For the SPD, it would therefore not be particularly credible to attack Merkel on the refugee issue. It had its hands doubly tied up.

The SPD then decided to nominate Martin Schulz as its top candidate for chancellor. Schulz had been an active politician at the level of the European Union. In particular, he had served as president of the European Parliament, and in that role, he was well respected. He had, however, not been engaged in national politics in Germany for almost two decades. I always say that it is best to launch a campaign as a free man. In that sense, it was a strike of liberation for the SPD to nominate someone that had not personally been part of the incumbent government. Schulz was elected with a stunning 100 percent of the vote as the new party leader and chancellor candidate, a score that only illustrates to what degree the party base desired a new face and messenger who was independent from the incumbent government. Instead of taking the party out of the grand coalition prison, Schulz quickly became part of it. After the election, the German magazine *Der Spiegel* published an inside report of Schulz's campaign. Apparently, the SPD had internal research showing that voters would not like Schulz, a man, to attack Merkel, a woman.[100] I agree that such a situation would certainly have required Schulz to be extra careful and respectful, but the question for me is clearly *how* to go on the offense to show contrast, not whether or not to do so. We said earlier that a challenger has to make the case for why the incumbent needs to be replaced and how they could do better. Both arguments cannot be made without showing contrast.

I think that the SPD made the mistake of using survey research to answer an expert question. There's a parallel here to the point I made earlier regarding policy specifics. When asked directly, voters will always say that they do not like negative campaigns, but that does not mean that negative campaigns are not effective. There's a good chance that voters will dislike what you tell them about your opponent even more than they dislike the fact that you're saying it. It's important to clarify, though, that I am not advocating smear tactics. US-style attack ads that directly accuse the opponent of something probably do not work in many other countries, and the "hit job" must be done indirectly in such cultures. Election campaigns are nonetheless about showing lines of distinction with respect to policy, big ideas, character, and the style of governing, which Schulz was unwilling or unable to do. As the campaign went along, things turned into a total disaster for the SPD and its top candidate. On election day, it got 20.5 percent of the vote. Coming from a low level of support in the previous election, it lost another 5.2 percent and reached the lowest level ever.[101]

If you look at it from the perspective of the voters, the result makes sense: except for tradition, why should anybody vote for the SPD if there is no difference between the SPD and the CDU? Speaking of the CDU, it lost a brutal 8.6 percent of its own vote and landed at 32.9 percent. The result clearly reminds us of the vulnerability of the Merkel-led CDU. The main beneficiaries were the AfD and the Free Democratic Party, *Freie Demokratische Partei* (FDP), two parties on the right of the political spectrum who had offered contrast and an alternative for voters.

What could Schulz and the SPD have done differently? Honestly, there is no obvious, easy solution, but they should have tried to find a way to show contrast. If they could not disagree with Merkel on the principle of Germany accepting refugees, then they could have criticized Merkel for doing so without much of a plan. It is also important for challengers to keep in mind in such a situation what I mentioned at the beginning of this chapter—you are not (yet) running the country. In other words, you are not required to have a full-fledged solution for every problem facing the country. Do not burden yourself unnecessarily.

Another example revealing dangerous traps for challengers is Democrat John Kerry, who ran for president of the US in 2004, challenging then-incumbent Republican president George W. Bush. This case provides intriguing insights into what it is like to run as a challenger, as I discovered while interviewing several people involved in the campaign as part of my dissertation research. Kerry was not necessarily unwilling, but he was rather unable to show contrast. One of the main issues at the time was the war in Iraq, which had started after the terrorist attacks of 9/11. As I wrote earlier, the military intervention was rather popular at the beginning, but when it was time for

George W. Bush to run for reelection, this had noticeably changed. The American people had started to tire of the war as its human and financial cost was rising, with no end in sight. While the issue of the war was a liability and weakness for the incumbent president, the challenger seemed unable to draw contrast and was therefore also unable to take advantage of that weakness. This is surprising given the fact that Kerry had served during the Vietnam War and was a decorated war hero; one would think that this should be an issue that is a strength for him. Part of the problem was that as a senator, John Kerry had voted in favor of authorizing President Bush to take military action against Iraq. During the campaign, Kerry also maintained that his vote at the time was correct, and that he would do it again. The original reason given by Bush to go to war in Iraq was that the country had weapons of mass destruction. Even when it became clear that there were no weapons of mass destruction and that Iraq had been no imminent threat to the US, Kerry still insisted that voting for the authorization had been the right thing at the time. In other words, it was not clear what Kerry would do differently from Bush. He ran ads trying to explain his position, but it became so complicated that it took minutes to clarify it without showing much contrast and without a clear takeaway for voters. "If you're explaining, you're losing" is commonly said in our industry and turned out to be the case for John Kerry.[102]

POLITICAL VACCINATION: HOW TO NEUTRALIZE ANY WEAKNESSES

Every candidate has weaknesses. The differentiating factor among candidates is that smart ones do something about it. The first step in that respect is to be brutally honest about this in the internal assessment. Only if we are candid about weaknesses can we then deal with them in an effective manner, neutralize them, or even turn them into strengths. Typical weaknesses can be to be considered as too extreme (to the left or to the right of the political spectrum), to be too young or too old, or to lack experience or awareness. Some candidates have a small political base, limited appeal beyond the base, or no base at all. Yet other candidates have skeletons in their closet, meaning sins in their previous political, business, or private lives that risk becoming an issue during a campaign.

During my time in Washington, DC, at the Graduate School of Political Management, Dr. Ronald Faucheux taught me the concept of *inoculation* in politics. Basically, this means that as a campaign, you take a series of strategic measures to neutralize your weaknesses.[103] This is one of the things that should be done long before the election because it takes time for it to take effect and to be credible for voters. Let us take age, for example. Candidates are occasionally accused of being too young or too old for an office. I have worked for a governor who was only thirty-four years old and a mayor of a city with more than a million voters who was past eighty years old. I have also tested age several times in focus groups and found that voters usually do not perceive someone as too young or too old to serve per se. The key for them is to see that the candidate in question can perform the job. Faucheux explained that an inoculation strategy for an older candidate, therefore, might include pictures and footage that show the candidate in action. Such a candidate would be seen as vital and dynamic. There should also be a youth campaign for that candidate and footage of him being surrounded by young people. A common prejudice is that old people talk a lot about the past. An elder candidate should make an explicit effort to talk about the future and champion futuristic issues such as technology or digitization. An inoculation strategy in such a case would also include paying particular attention to debate and interview preparation. If an elder candidate stumbles, does not hear a question, or mixes up facts, it would easily confirm a concern that voters might already have. It would therefore be important to invest the time and practice necessary to try and minimize such incidents from happening. I remember discussing this once with the team of a senior senator running for reelection, for whom I was working. "You're old, you're old. Not much you can do about it," his son said. As I just explained, I disagree. There are plenty of things that can be done to neutralize how this is being perceived, and the same can be done about any other potential weakness.

As another example, I have worked for a gubernatorial candidate whom we expected to be attacked for not hailing from the area. We made sure that his proposals would be tailor-made to the local area, showing a deep understanding of local problems and offering solutions on how to fix them. The area included known and beautiful tourist spots, and he promised to introduce a discounted rate for locals to visit them. At the end of a hard-fought campaign, my client won a narrow victory.

In many European countries, there is an increasing call for female leaders. Particularly in a green or leftist party, being a man can be a disadvantage. You might wonder what one can do about his biological gender, and I answer that with respect to an inoculation strategy—there is a whole lot one can do. I had a client in Switzerland who was in such a situation, and I advised him to, first of all, embrace and vote for typical women's issues such as equal pay for equal work. He should then have a support group composed entirely of women and its members would give testimonials for him. He should reach out to all important female leaders from his party in his district and campaign for them, raise money for them, and have an ongoing dialogue with them. He agreed with my plan, implemented it with discipline, and won.

EXPERIENCE IS BECOMING LESS IMPORTANT

One of the most common accusations against a challenger is a lack of necessary experience to run the city, province, or country. As the examples of Zelensky and Macron illustrate, experience as a criterion has lost much of its importance to voters. As a rule of thumb, I think that the more voters are unhappy with the status quo, the more they are willing to take a risk and the less experience will matter. Long before Donald Trump, Texas businessman Ross Perot ran for president of the US. In the debates, he famously tried to turn his lack of political experience into an advantage by making a joke about it. "I don't have any experience in running up a $4 trillion debt. I don't have any experience in gridlock government, where nobody takes responsibility for anything and everybody blames everybody else," he said.[104] When Hillary Clinton was running against Donald Trump, her main pitch was that she was uniquely qualified to become president. When Barack Obama was campaigning for her, the message was always that no candidate—not himself, and not her husband, Bill Clinton—had ever been better prepared to move into the Oval Office.[105] While that may have been true, voters were not primarily looking for experience at that time. According to the CNN exit polls, Clinton won 90 percent of the voters who said that the right experience was the candidate quality that mattered most to them. That group of voters, however, only made up 22 percent of the electorate. The candidate quality that mattered most to voters was "who can bring change" with 39 percent.[106] In other words, selling Clinton with experience was a mismatch between political demand and offer. It is like a waiter trying to convince you that the restaurant has the best steak after you told him that you want to eat fish.

This does not mean that experience has become immaterial for voters. I look at it like a threshold, meaning that a candidate needs to convince voters that he is able to do the job. Once a candidate passes that threshold, other criteria become more important. We are definitely no longer in a situation where more experience is automatically better. In fact, the world is changing at such a fast pace nowadays that a relatively younger leader might be even better equipped to deal with current challenges in the voters' eyes. In that respect, the case of

Sebastian Kurz, who became chancellor of Austria at the age of the thirty-one, is particularly interesting. You might wonder how Kurz was able to pass that threshold given his young age. Well, prior to running for chancellor, Kurz had served as secretary of foreign affairs. At that time, the refugee crisis was a big issue. Kurz took a clear stand and was instrumental in closing a major route through which asylum seekers came to Europe. The stand was highly popular with voters, and by taking decisive action, Kurz was able to pass the threshold in the eyes of many voters.

With respect to experience, it is also important to differentiate between political experience in the sense of serving in a public office and campaign experience. Donald Trump in the US and Volodymyr Zelensky in Ukraine are interesting examples in that respect. As mentioned, they had never run for office, and both had close to zero political experience when they launched their candidacies. That said, they were both eminently experienced with respect to the media. Donald Trump had mastered the art of provocation and knew exactly what kind of media attention his statements would give him. As an actor, Zelensky was great at behaving in front of the camera. So, in terms of campaign skills, both were not as inexperienced as one might think. In fact, they had better campaign skills than many established politicians. When Bob Dole, for example, ran for president in 1996 to challenge incumbent Bill Clinton, he had spent almost thirty years as a senator. As the Republican leader in the Senate, he was without any doubt a tremendously experienced lawmaker, but that did not necessarily make him a good candidate. In fact, quite the opposite was true. He was rather uncomfortable giving a speech, did not come across particularly well on television, and lacked practice in candidate debates. Having not had a competitive election in years, he entered the race totally unprepared with respect to campaign skills.

DIVIDED PARTIES RARELY WIN GREAT ELECTORAL VICTORIES

While incumbents often have their parties under control and are set as the top candidate, the situation is different for challengers. They have to establish themselves as the (main opposition) candidate first. In the US, there are primary elections where the candidates of the same party compete for votes, run television ads attacking each other directly, and face off at debates. In other countries, party members or party boards decide on who will be the standard-bearer. In such a case, the intraparty competition is more subtle. Either way, it is crucial for a party to unify once a candidate is chosen. While this book is not about nomination contests, I want to press this point about coming together once the designation is made. Regardless of the political system, intraparty competition has the potential to do lasting damage to the prevailing candidate. It has often been said that this was the case after the 2016 Democratic primary, when Hillary Clinton beat Bernie Sanders for the nomination. Clinton was never able to fully convince Sanders's supporters that she had won the nomination fair and square. When Clinton later narrowly lost the general election to Trump, it was said that disappointed Bernie voters either stayed home or even supported Trump and thereby contributed to Trump's upset victory.

It doesn't have to be that way. Competition can actually be an advantage that will further help challengers to maximize their advantages. It can force them to build an organization, network, database, and fundraising machine that they might otherwise not build and to campaign in areas that they would ignore in other circumstances. It can also attract tremendous media attention, but it all depends on how the candidates and the party leadership handle the situation. I tell all my clients after they win the nomination that the first thing they should do is to reach out to the loser. A positive example of this is when Ronald Reagan ran for president in 1980. After a hard-fought primary campaign, Reagan nominated his rival for the nomination,

George H. W. Bush, as his vice presidential candidate. If you don't want to go that far, I still recommend that you showcase your reaching out. Voters will always doubt whether this is for real, so don't hesitate to exaggerate a bit. Many candidates unfortunately don't want to do that, and I think that the true reason for it is because of pride. They wonder why they should reach out since they just won the nomination. It's a missed opportunity because the person who lost the nomination contest to you has a unique credibility to endorse you for the general election. It's also clear to me that it's incumbent on the winner to reach out to the loser and that this is in the interest of everyone. The one who lost the nomination doesn't want to look like a sore loser and be held responsible if the party loses the election. As for the winner, coming together is an absolute prerequisite to build an even bigger alliance because divided parties rarely win great electoral victories.

A great example of this was when François Hollande ran for president of France in 2012. It was the first time that the Socialist Party nominated its standard-bearer through an internal primary. The two finalists were Martine Aubry, the first secretary of the Socialist Party at the time, and François Hollande, the former first secretary of the Socialist Party. When the results came in, and it was clear that Hollande had won, Aubry immediately recognized her loss. She welcomed the winner in the party headquarters in order to demonstrate that there wouldn't be any fracture and no time would be wasted to go after the incumbent.

Another instructive case is when Gerhard Schröder, the former chancellor of Germany, first became the top candidate of his party, the SPD. Back at the time, two men wanted to be the party's top candidate for the nationwide elections: Schröder, who was the prime minister from the state of Lower Saxony, and Oskar Lafontaine, the chairman of the SPD. The two were vicious competitors and deeply distrusted each other, but they also knew that they needed each other to ultimately reach their goal. Lafontaine had brutally lost a nationwide election before and knew that Schröder had broader appeal to centrist swing voters. Schröder, on the other hand, knew that Lafontaine had the support of most party leaders and the rank-and-file members of the party, for whom Schröder was too moderate in his positions. It so happened that in the spring, a few months before the nationwide election, voters in Lower Saxony were scheduled to head to the polls for their local statewide election. In other words, Gerhard Schröder would be up for reelection as prime minister in his home state of Lower Saxony only a few months before the nationwide election would take place. It was therefore decided that the party would reach the decision on the designation of the top candidate for the national elections only after the local elections in Lower Saxony. Both aspirants agreed that if Schröder won in Lower Saxony, he would be the candidate for chancellor. If Schröder lost, on the other hand, Lafontaine would be the candidate. The agreement turned the local election in Lower Saxony into a US-style primary, and the competition between the two attracted tremendous media attention.

On election day in Lower Saxony, the SPD won a stunning 47.9 percent of the vote, which was a gain of 3.6 percent compared with the previous election.[107] On the same night, Lafontaine addressed reporters that had gathered outside of his home. I remember watching on TV when he stepped outside of his house, offered the journalists a shot of liquor to celebrate the "nice win in Lower Saxony," and announced that he would ask the party leadership council to designate Schröder as the SPD candidate for chancellor.

During the general election campaign, Schröder and Lafontaine campaigned as a team, similar to a presidential candidate and his running mate in the US. The slogan was "innovation and social justice." Lafontaine represented social justice, appealing to the party base. Schröder, on the other hand, represented innovation and appealed to centrist voters who simply wanted a new leadership. During the campaign, the setup was carried out with great discipline and allowed the SPD to take full advantage of the challenger status, and on election day, it won a historic victory.

LAST PIECE OF ADVICE

A big-city mayor and longtime client of mine once told me that there is no king without a kingdom. I absolutely agree. Maximizing the advantages of the challenger also means maximizing the votes you can get from your home base, your stronghold, your kingdom. Whether your base is a geographically defined area, a sociodemographic subgroup of the electorate, or an ideological or religious base, do not take these votes for granted but milk them to the maximum. A friend of mine once ran for *Ständerat*, which is the upper house of the Swiss parliament, an equivalent to the Senate in the US. I emphasize that she was a friend and not a client. In fact, I have never worked for a friend during my seventeen years running my own business, and that is probably why I still have most of them. My friend fought a highly contested election against another heavyweight. On election day, she received 49.4 percent of the vote and lost by 3,637 votes.[108] I remember how she commented on her loss in the media by saying that she could have found those lacking 3,637 votes in her neighborhood (which heavily favored her). It is true, and what is true for her is true for most other candidates: if you lose a close race, you could have found the missing votes in your kingdom.

6

BECOME THE BEST CAMPAIGNER EVER

If you want to run for office, then welcome to the people business. The politicians with the best campaign skills I have seen also have great people skills. This is true when dealing with crowds but equally true when dealing with people one-on-one. Outstanding politicians can electrify their audience, come across pleasantly from the television to the living room, and make each and every person around them feel special. Challengers often benefit from long and intense campaigns as it gives them time to make up for deficiencies such as, for example, lower awareness. If you are running as an opposition candidate, you therefore have to be willing and able to launch a state-of-the-art campaign operation and develop your campaign skills. This chapter provides practical advice on how to get there, increase your media presence, give superb speeches, prepare to win debates, use social media to your advantage, and assemble a top-notch campaign team. Chances are you will need all these resources to win.

Campaigns are truly unique to politicians. If you think about it, bureaucrats and business leaders have power, academics and journalists can be right or wrong, but only politicians run election campaigns as candidates and submit themselves to the verdict of voters. In fact, the impression of campaigns is what attracts a great deal of politicians to politics. If you ask politicos what originally enticed them into politics, it is usually either family roots or a landmark campaign. While some politicians love the fame and media aspect of campaigns, others like the retail politics of shaking hands and kissing babies. When things go well, the ego boost you get from an election campaign is similar to the one an athlete must feel after a big win. A client of mine who was running for president had close to a million people cheering at him in his final rally before clinching victory. How thrilling that must feel.

Certainly, the personality of the (top) candidate really matters in campaigns. This is true even with respect to polarizing figures who often fit and represent their respective countries incredibly well. It is no surprise that Silvio Berlusconi was prime minister of Italy and a dominating figure in Italian politics for decades, yet a joke of his is being misunderstood in another country. If Donald Trump were born as a German, he might have done some lucrative real estate deals in Frankfurt, but I doubt he would have ascended the party hierarchy (of any party for that matter) in Berlin. If born as an American citizen, on the other hand, Angela Merkel would maybe have become a professor of chemistry at Harvard University, but I doubt she would have been elected to the White House. In other words, the life stories, attitudes, and demeanor of candidates, the way they speak, and their ability to connect with the electorate of a given country at large really matter.

CHARISMA CAN BE LEARNED

When discussing the appeal of a candidate, pundits and journalists often use the word "charisma." A synonym would probably be presence or aura and, yes, some people are more naturally appealing than others. If you feel that you are at a disadvantage here, I have good news for you: charisma can be learned. Bill Clinton, for example, is one of the living politicians with the greatest campaign skills ever. When I shook his hand as a young student years ago at an event in Washington, DC, it felt every bit as it had been described by journalists. For a second, I had the impression that his entire focus was on me, and it was electrifying. Clinton is also an engaging speaker and formidable debater, and yet few people thought of him as charismatic back in 1988. That year, Clinton delivered his first major speech at a Democratic National Convention when he was supposed to introduce the presidential candidate, Michael Dukakis. Unfortunately, he somehow got lost in a long speech, which bored his audience.[109] The words "in closing" drew the biggest round of applause.[110] It was brutal and humiliating. At that moment, few people would probably have thought that only four years later, Bill Clinton would be the Democratic presidential nominee himself. Clinton was able to recover by taking action and by taking a risk. Shortly after the convention speech, he managed to appear on *The Tonight Show*, at the time the number one late-night talk show. In 1988, it was a new thing for a politician to appear on such a show. Clinton convinced the audience by showing a humorous side and making self-deprecating jokes.[111] The boring convention speech was soon forgotten, and winning the presidency twice only further boosted his charisma.

At the local level, I have worked for a mayor who was seen as aloof and distant. In order to change that, we used key events in the city to showcase a more likable and warm personality. The mayor also made a conscious effort to smile when chatting with citizens and he participated in outdoor happenings. Over time, I noticed that comments about him in focus groups changed. While voters had always appreciated his work and leadership, they now also liked the person.

The takeaway here is that if you want to become a great campaigner, you have to want to continuously improve your campaign skills. The way to do that is to get out of your comfort zone and become better at the things you don't like or aren't particularly gifted in. While this might be easy to read about, it will be emotionally different if you have to do it for yourself. Working on your campaign skills is also something that cannot be delegated. You have to be willing to do it yourself and to invest the necessary time. As entrepreneur and author Jim Rohn says, "you can't hire someone else to do your push-ups for you."[112] You may hire a personal trainer who can make your efforts more effective, but you will have to do the exercises yourself.

An interesting example in that respect is Luiz Inácio "Lula" da Silva from Brazil, who I mentioned in chapter 4 about the secrets of selling change. After three consecutive losses, he decided to do things differently on his fourth attempt. While he was already a seasoned politician by that time, he invested considerable time and attention into becoming a better campaigner and continues to reap the benefits from that effort. As discussed earlier, Lula started with the physical aspect of looking the part. These things matter, and they matter more nowadays. As the news cycle has become nonstop and in the time of social media and constant selfies, style and aesthetics have become even more important. I have, for example, tested the issue of being overweight several times in focus groups. While it can be dealt with and voters do not always hold it against a candidate, on its face, it's negative. If you know that you have to lose weight, lose it before the start of the campaign. Taking drastic action like this sends voters a strong signal of personal will and readiness. A good example of this is Joschka Fischer, a German politician from the Green Party. He lost thirty kilograms within ten months and became a passionate runner. He went on to become Germany's minister of foreign affairs and the most popular member of the government at the time.

That said, there are sometimes things that you cannot improve, or no matter how much you improve, you will never be at eye level with your opponent. The way to deal with such a situation is not to blindly accept the metrics of your competition or the media but to change them. When José María Aznar challenged Prime Minister Felipe González in Spain, for example, he was in such circumstances. Aznar, a former tax inspector, was seen as aloof and as no match for incumbent González in terms of charisma. Instead of competing on the incumbent's turf, he turned things around. "Spain has had enough charisma," he claimed and defeated the incumbent.[113]

THE IMPORTANCE OF THE MEDIA

If you are running for a high-profile office, chances are that most voters will never see you in person but instead in the media. Successful candidates, therefore, take the media seriously, make themselves available to journalists, and give the campaign the attention, time, and preparation it deserves. For some politicians, this is a no-brainer. They instantly get the importance of the media and enjoy it a lot. In fact, some politicians literally crave and need the media limelight, while others prefer the personal interaction with the voters at rallies. For them, the media is an unpleasant sideshow. I remember my early days in the trenches working for a candidate who was running for a nationwide office. We had to shoot a TV ad very early in the morning because he had rallies scheduled all day long. I think that the order of priorities is wrong here, and yet it happens all the time. While physical presence can be an important factor in local campaigns, mass media is a far more effective way to reach voters in a nationwide campaign. It is quite obvious to me that no matter how hard you try, the number of voters you can meet in person in a nationwide election is seriously limited. Call it retail and wholesale, but maybe I say that because I cannot imagine the ego boost candidates get out of a cheering crowd.

Be that as it may, the media can be a crucial advantage if a challenger uses it wisely. Counterintuitively, the performance of seasoned politicians often gets worse over time. Even politicians who once were natural talents when dealing with the media, after some time in power, often become less accessible, crankier, and easily irritated with the journalists.

In general terms, I suggest looking at your media effort making the following distinctions:

- *Earned media*: as a campaign, you try to get positive media coverage.
- *Paid media*: advertising on television, radio, billboards or other.
- *Social media*: it can be earned or paid in nature, but since it is so distinct, I nevertheless treat it as an entirely separate category.
- *Owned media*: media you own and control, such as a blog or a party magazine. In some cases, politicians also own TV channels, radio stations, or newspapers.

Most campaigns are a mix of these, and as mentioned, the patterns of media consumption have greatly changed over the past years. As a result, campaigns increasingly have to play the whole field.

EARNED MEDIA: HOW TO DRAMATICALLY INCREASE YOUR MEDIA PRESENCE

At the top of the wish list of virtually all my clients (other than winning the election) is to increase their media presence. Indeed, positive media coverage is the wind at your back when running for office. It helps raise your awareness among voters, builds up your credibility among those who already know you, and helps with fundraising. The advantage of earned media is that it is free, and it is also often more credible than paid advertising.*

---

* In some developing countries, it is common practice to pay journalists for coverage, but such bribes are not what I am talking about in this section.

The downside is that you have less control over it. You are invited onto a talk show or not, you get covered in the news or not. If you do get media attention, journalists have their own agenda when doing their job. They balance ideals such as journalistic integrity and serving the public good against selfish interests such as wanting to build their reputation and advance their career. Always coloring their choices is the need to satisfy the fundamental demand of the media outlet that pays their salary; that is, what they report has to help sell newspapers, increase TV ratings, and generate ad revenue for the company. Therefore, you the candidate must accept that the journalist, not you, decides what questions to ask you and what snippets of your answers to show on the evening news.

Politicians and candidates who spend their time complaining about the allegedly "fake" or "biased" media (i.e., stories the candidates don't like) are a dime a dozen. Do not adopt this narrative, because it will definitely not increase your media presence. No journalist has to cover you, let alone cover you the way you want. What is important to you might not be considered newsworthy for journalists. As a consequence, you have to present your input in a way that is relevant to the media. The good news is that if you give journalists what they want, when they want it, it is easy to gain a foothold with the media. I know because I've done it numerous times. I have been on the front page of several newspapers in my country; have sat for unedited, live television interviews in three languages; and have had my guest articles published in numerous countries including the US, France, Germany, Japan, Finland, the Philippines, and the Czech Republic. If I can build mutually beneficial relationships with the media, so can you.

That is to say, your earned media work has to start with the right attitude. You have to look at interactions with journalists as a fair exchange among peers where you give as much as you get. Journalists need information, content, and juicy stories to feed their media outlets, and that's what you are giving them. The media is mostly interested in attention-grabbing news, conflict, and scandals. To be the first one to report a story is tremendously important for reporters, as is insight information about what happens in closed-door meetings. Fame also works well, and occasionally, expertise is in demand. If you want to increase your media presence, you have to package your message in one of these ways. Also keep in mind that journalists work under tremendous time constraints and increasingly also under financial pressure. There has been much downsizing among editorial staff in the recent past. Oftentimes, journalists are young and their political and historical knowledge is limited. If you can put yourself in the journalist's shoes, think like a journalist, and package and deliver a story to them on a silver platter, it can go a long way in improving your earned media opportunities with them in the future. This demonstrates that you understand the pressures they face, the deliverables they seek, and the mutual benefit of media coverage. I do not mean to sound cynical here, but this can also be an advantage in your media work. I have written entire interviews myself (questions and answers) that were printed in reputable newspapers with important circulation.

Another important key to increase your media presence is to actively pitch yourself to journalists. You have to build a network of journalists with whom you interact, to whom you actively offer stories, and who will, over time, also contact you as a source for their pieces. Depending on the stage of your career in public service, your opportunities will greatly vary, but no matter where you are, you should know at least one journalist. Think about which journalist you know the best. Then think about a story that you could pitch to them: Do you plan to block a bill in parliament (conflict)? Are you introducing an important amendment on a current topic (heads-up)? Do you serve on the health committee during a time of a pandemic (expertise)?

If nothing else is getting you coverage, the easiest way to get publicity for any politician is to go against the leadership of your own party. You may pay a high political price for this coverage, but if you threaten to not support a proposal introduced by your party or break with a long-standing narrative, journalists will want to know why and write about it.

When building your network of trusted journalists, here are some guidelines to consider:

- Journalists like politicians who are easily accessible. So, when journalists call, treat it as a priority. Do not hesitate to give them your cell phone number for direct access.
- Try not to be high maintenance. Politicians who want to rephrase or reshoot without changing anything substantially, or those who complain about every little detail, quickly earn a reputation among fellow journalists as being difficult to deal with.
- Adapt to the tone, style, and vocabulary of the media in question. Some like it short and catchy, while others look for more substance.
- Don't take it personally when your story or guest article is being turned down. It often has more to do with the media outlet's internal situation at the moment than with the story or article you are pitching. I have been in a situation where I pitched a story for a client and was refused, not because the story was bad, but simply because there was no space. On other occasions, a story I found mediocre was played really big because they needed something at that point in time.

Once you have the attention of the media, the challenge is that journalists are usually not going to be interested in your campaign message. It takes some skill and creativity to combine the headlines of the day with your campaign message. Some politicians, such as George W. Bush, for example, are naturally good at this. Whether it was during his campaigns in Texas for governor or later at the national level, once the message was decided, Bush would stick to it. Not his opponent, not hostile questioning by a reporter, and not even a heckler could make him depart from it. I remember how he would occasionally even talk about himself in the third person as the messenger. Other candidates have to train for such message discipline. If this is your case, then obtain media training to practice staying on message when faced with tough questions.

A common advice for writers is, "get to the point, make the point, repeat the point." I totally agree, and it is also a good guideline for political candidates, who often underestimate how much repetition it takes until a message sinks in among voters. Think about it from the voters' perspective: they do not get up in the morning and look for what their politicians said or did recently. Instead, voters are busy running their own lives, going to work, paying their bills, and raising their children. It is not because you put out a press release or hold a press conference that all voters will know what you said in that release or conference. Candidates, therefore, have to be willing and able to repeat their own message at the point of being bored themselves.

Keeping a candidate disciplined can also be a key challenge for those handling and advising a candidate. This was, for example, the case with Donald Trump, who certainly had a good feeling for what his audience wanted to hear but is known for being an undisciplined messenger on the campaign trail. In that respect, it is an interesting detail that the now-famous idea of the wall between the US and Mexico was apparently invented to keep Trump focused on the issue of immigration. It's been said that he was rather lukewarm about the idea at the beginning but tested it out at an early campaign event. When the crowd went through the roof, the wall soon became a centerpiece of Trump's speeches and the entire campaign.[114]

PAID MEDIA: WHAT MAKES A GREAT POLITICAL AD

It happens regularly that clients show me their advertising and ask me whether or not I "like" it. I find this amusing. It is not a question of like, but whether the advertising, what paid media essentially equates to, moves votes into your corner. Earlier, we said that the message is a key component of a campaign—and in that sense, the main purpose of an ad is to communicate that message to your target audience coherently and with oomph. The fact that you have total control over the content is the main advantage of paid media. Advertising also allows you to communicate with voters who do not care much about politics. If you are appearing on the news, that is great, but you are only communicating to those who want to watch the news. It's often the less-informed and less-engaged people, however, who decide an election.

I do not buy into the argument that is sometimes made that television advertising has lost its impact. While it is not as dominant as it used to be since patterns of media consumption are changing, TV is still the ace of political advertising in most countries. If you are legally allowed to run TV ads, and your financial situation permits it, I would strongly argue that you do so. In the US, the relentless airing of paid television commercials is the heart of most election campaigns. In other countries, the possibilities for political campaigns to purchase airtime is more regulated and limited. In Brazil and some European countries, candidates are given TV airtime for free. In Germany, for example, parties are given time on the public networks, which are widely watched throughout the country, and in addition, candidates can buy airtime on the private networks. In a country where that is not available, a campaign has no choice but to use other tools. In my home country of Switzerland, for example, political advertising on television and radio is banned. As a result, campaigns resort to ads in newspapers and billboards.

The problem is that many ads are done poorly, whether TV commercials, print ads, or other forms of advertising. What I mean by this is that they sound and feel like, well, political advertising. I sometimes experience this when I work in a country where I do not understand the local language. By simply looking at the visuals and by listening to the voiceover, I can feel that it is blatant propaganda. Here are a few key points to remember on how to avoid this and create effective political ads:

- Less is more. A political ad is not the place for a laundry list; it should strongly deliver one main point.
- The goal is not to create art or to win a creativity contest. While an ad has to be executed in a visually appealing way and may well include some eye candy, the main point of the visuals is to communicate the message.
- Think about your ad campaign as a series of ads. Great advertising campaigns rarely consist of one knockout punch.
- Voters are not stupid. It is therefore important for an ad not to talk down to voters. I am skeptical about ads that are limited to mere endorsements, entertainment, and celebrities. Also, interactions with voters should be genuine and believable.
- Keep an eye on the production costs. I have witnessed many times how advertising agencies lured politicians into creating expensive ads with many actors and special effects. I wondered why, because based on what voters told us in the focus groups, simple straight-talking ads with content were more effective. After some time, I found out that the agencies were compensated with a percentage of the total cost.
- Give the medicine some time to work. As a rule of thumb, an ad has to air at least three weeks on prime time before making an impact. Many politicians make the mistake of assuming or hoping for an impact too fast. As a result, their approach

becomes an erratic shotgun attack with ads and messages constantly changing.

Ideally, you would test advertising material in focus groups *before* running it and spending serious money on it. It seems like a no-brainer to me, and yet it happens all the time that candidates are so excited about their own ads that they do not bother testing them. I have worked for a senatorial candidate who was such a case. By the time we finally tested his ad, we found that the ad actually cost him votes. When voters in the focus groups first learned about his previous record, they liked him, and it converted into votes. Once voters were exposed to his ad, however, they were so annoyed that they took back their votes. Ouch! As a more positive example, I have been in a situation where respondents said that the ad we tested gives them goose bumps. That is precisely how the ads matched their feelings and demands.

HOW TO USE SOCIAL MEDIA TO YOUR ADVANTAGE

I once worked for a client who had a business background and wanted to run for Congress. We had a first session before the Christmas break and then were set to meet again in the new year. During the holidays, he zealously opened profiles and accounts on various social media apps. When we met again, he asked me, what should I do on social media? Good question.

Before I answer that question, let me say that the impact of social media in election campaigns is greatly overestimated. I post weekly on my two blogs, one in English and one in German. I am daily tweeting out two takeaways about the art and science of election campaigns and I have more than twenty-five hundred followers on Facebook. At the time of writing, I have more than fourteen hundred connections on LinkedIn, most of whom are opinion leaders, politicians, and journalists, which makes my profile among the top 15 percent of my industry according to LinkedIn (and I assume there are some real social media champions in my industry). This being said, let me repeat: the impact of social media in election campaigns is greatly overestimated. Ever since it became public that Cambridge Analytica, an online data firm, worked for Donald Trump's upset win in 2016 and the Brexit campaign, journalists love the story of powerful, secret forces that supposedly impact campaigns online. Similarly, politicians are fascinated by social media, foremost because it is cheaper than traditional advertising. They are also attracted to the siren song of a social media campaign because they think it would not require much work. In their minds, things would go viral without much effort and sweat. They are dreaming. It is also quite obvious to me that the people who gush about the power of social media campaigns are almost exclusively the people who make a living selling social media campaigns. There is little independent academic research supporting their claim.

To begin with, the Internet's penetration varies from country to country. That is usually one of the things I test in the survey when I start to work in a new place. I was involved in several developing countries, and it is often about half of the voters who are online daily or several times a day. So, yes, social media may be a factor politicians should use to communicate with that half of the electorate, but they should also not forget that the other half of voters are not regularly online. Even in countries with high Internet penetration, this does not mean that people use it for political purposes. A good friend of mine is running a business for eyelash extensions, and Instagram is the pivot point of the business: marketing, advertising, booking appointments, and referring clients are all done on the app. Similarly, the younger and more urban the target audience of your campaign is, the bigger a role social media will play. In the case of a senior senator in a rural state running for (his last) reelection, however, social media will likely be less decisive. Or said differently, old rural people vote. While they are often underrepresented online, they are certainly important in politics.

One of the most prominent examples of a politician using social media is Donald Trump. Having more than eighty million followers, with whom you can communicate without a media filter and for free, is precious political capital. Trump was successful on social media because he was authentic and willing to say things his voters were thinking but other politicians wouldn't dare to say. In other words, he was not afraid to put out, defend, and double down on controversial statements. The case of Donald Trump, though, also shows how dangerous it is to build your house on rented land. Social media platforms can change their rules anytime, and when Twitter banned him, Trump lost a major outlet. Even before his profiles were shut down, he paid a heavy price for his social media activity as he is perhaps the most polarizing politician on earth. While he does have a base of enthusiastic supporters, many other voters see him negatively. When he first got elected, he was the president-elect with the highest negative rating of all time. According to the MSNBC exit polls, he had a 60 percent unfavorable rating on the day he was elected president.[115] Four years later, he became the first incumbent president in twenty-eight years to lose reelection. Imagine the hostility he faces on a daily basis. Are you and your family willing to pay that price for the eighty million followers? It would also be wrong to attribute Trump's success in winning the Republican nomination and the general election in 2016 to social media alone. It certainly played a role, but Trump also benefited from massive earned media because of his personality, style, and message.

From a historic and structural point of view, it is also nothing new that technological innovations impact campaigns. As I mentioned in the introduction, the advent of radio changed campaigns because candidates could all of a sudden communicate with voters in different places at the same time. One could argue that the pace at which technology is developing and therefore impacting campaigns has sharply increased, but make no mistake, technological changes do not change the fundamentals of campaigns. The new tool does not replace the message and should never be the message itself.

In other words, social media has to fit into your overall campaign plan. From a strategic point of view, you are basically doing two things in an election campaign. You are trying to convince voters who are undecided or leaning softly toward you, or you are trying to mobilize your own supporters in order to maximize their turnout on election day. Social media is a precious tool for the latter; it helps to do the traditional mobilizing in a more systematic and interactive way. Successful opposition candidates such as Obama, Zelensky, or Macron often launch important grassroots operations that sometimes become real grassroots movements, and social media (and technology more broadly) can help you accomplish that. Here are some guidelines on how to use and leverage social media in election campaigns:

> *Social media is for people, not organizations*: People perform much better on social media than organizations. Therefore, it should be the tool of the top candidate, not the party.
>
> *Social media cannot be delegated*: The key on social media is to be authentic and real. If a candidate delegates it to someone down the hall, it loses much of its attractiveness. Social media works best if the top candidate is willing to build it up over a certain period of time. For this, Donald Trump is a good example because he really did tweet himself and let everyone know what crossed his mind at any time, day or night.
>
> *Give real content*: People want to get real news and see real content on social media. Behind-the-scenes shots are also great, for example.

Give exclusive content: In the US, it has become customary for candidates to make important announcements on social media. For example, presidential candidates would announce their vice presidential picks first on social media to their supporters instead of in a traditional press conference.

Social media is about creating controversy: Social media is driven by emotions, so controversy is crucial. People go on social media to express outrage or agree with something they already believe in. No one goes online to listen to different sides, weigh various opinions, and change their mind.

Do not look for recognition on social media: Many politicians look for instant gratification from voters, whether it is from real contact in rallies or online. Because of the controversial nature of social media, it is definitely the wrong place for that and it may even distort your perception and political gut feel.

Interact with your supporters: The advantage of social media is that you can interact with your supporters and ask them to do something for the campaign (write to friends, organize a neighborhood, donate). The goal is to use social media to turn supporters into volunteers and to organize and leverage their activities. In that sense, social media is best used in coordination with offline activism such as local campaign offices, voter contacts, or field operations.

The votes are in the list: Almost any expert on online business says that the money is in the email list. What they mean is that social media should be used to attract supporters and then find a reason to get their email address, from which something can be emailed and then sold to them. The equivalent for politics is that the votes are in the list. Give your followers a reason to give you their email address. Then start communicating with them via email. If you rely solely on social media, you are running the risk that the apps may change their rules and you will face the same fate of Donald Trump.

Be aware of bought traffic: In my experience, views, clicks, and followers that are bought and not organic are of really low quality. I usually tell clients to think about it the other way: have you ever clicked on a video that was suggested to you on Facebook? "Of course not," they usually reply. So, what makes you think that voters are so much dumber than you?

Use social media to get earned media: Another good way to use social media is not as a megaphone for your campaign but to communicate with journalists. In other words, it is used to get earned coverage in traditional media. Again, this is being done by stirring controversy that might be picked up by journalists. A variation of this is that if you avoid media interviews but create content on social media, you can try to influence what the media covers about your campaign (for lack of other choices).

Be aware of the time dump: All apps are created to make you addicted. So be aware of the time dump. The time investment should therefore be strictly limited. Also remember that attention is a zero-sum game.

Do not lose sight of the goal: Retweets and likes are not goals in themselves. The goal is to win the election, and in most countries, people vote offline. Whatever you do on social media must help you reach the goal. If people who can't vote for you like your stuff, you are fooling yourself. I remember a mayoral candidate in a city with more than one million voters who was bragging to me about the many followers he supposedly had on TikTok and how many influencers were supporting him. He lost the election in a landslide, as I had predicted to him after conducting one survey.

Never use social media after consuming alcohol: You may regret what you have tweeted or posted.

Never engage in a personal fight with a voter: Stay above the fray. If someone is rude, block them, but do not argue with a voter. It looks bad.

Now, look at your accounts and go through the checklist. How many of these guidelines are you following right now? As technology continues to develop, I think it is wise to observe, be innovative, and try out new things. In fact, every election cycle and every local or by-election should be used to try out new things and to measure their impact. That said, my observation is that the pace of innovation in social media has slowed down in recent times. If you think about it, the major apps we are using have been around for some years now, and not many new apps have established themselves on the market.

HOW TO WIN A DEBATE

Televised debates between the candidates have been a key component of US presidential campaigns for many decades. These debates have been emulated in local races, and during the past two or three decades, the format has been exported to many other countries that had not been familiar with them. Generally speaking, debates have the biggest impact in a country when they are new. Though quite some time ago in the US, much has been written in that respect about the 1960 presidential debate between John F. Kennedy and Richard

Nixon. It was the first debate at least partly seen on television, and people who watched it thought Kennedy won the debate. Among those voters who listened to it on the radio, however, a majority thought that Nixon won. Consequently, for your debate, remember that *how* things are being said—the demeanor and the visuals—is as important as *what* is actually being said. Voters generally like debates because they are the only opportunity to compare the candidates directly and next to each other. As a result, debates often have a large viewership and get important media coverage afterward.

There have been candidates who nevertheless refused to debate. Tony Blair from the UK did not debate his opponent, incumbent prime minister John Major, when he first ran. When Lula from Brazil ran for reelection as president, he also avoided debating his opponents during the first round of voting. When French president Jacques Chirac ran for reelection, he refused to debate Jean-Marie Le Pen, the right-wing candidate, against whom he faced off in the second round of voting. While Chirac argued that there is no debate possible with Le Pen's policies, I think that for most candidates who refused to debate, it was a political calculation. The potential downside outweighed the potential upside.

That's understandable because debates are tough. Candidates stand up there alone for ninety minutes or longer without the possibility to talk to a confidant, and weaknesses are easily exposed. One of the greatest examples of this is the second presidential debate during the 2016 Philippine election. One of the candidates had a dispute with the debate organizers, and as a result, the start of the debate was delayed. While the candidate in question and the debate organizers tried to sort things out, television was already broadcasting live. The other candidates stood in front of a nationwide TV audience, not doing anything. By solely standing there and trying to fill the gap, candidates displayed more to voters than if they would have given prepared answers to questions. Rodrigo Duterte, who ultimately won the race but at the time was a mayor, came across as chill, funny, and at ease with himself. He also seemed clear about his message and why he wanted to become president. While the other candidates seemed nervous and too hungry to get the position, he was the most authentic, and the voters rewarded it accordingly.[116]

The media and some observers often assess debates in superficial ways: How many minutes of applause? How many laughs? As a political consultant, I look at debates very differently. Dr. Faucheux, the professor I introduced earlier, correctly says that preparation for a debate should start with a definition of the strategic goals to accomplish.[117] Indeed, if you don't know what your strategic goal for the debate is, how can you assess afterward whether or not you were successful in a meaningful way? If you are ahead in the surveys, your minimum goal might simply be not to say or do anything that changes the dynamics of the race. If you are behind in the surveys by the time of the debate, on the other hand, your goal is to shake things up. In that case, you will probably have to go on the offense. Other strategic goals might be to address a particular attack in order to stop the bleeding; to show a different side to your personality; to drive home a key point about yourself, your opponent, or an issue; and by all means, to deliver your message. Part of the strategic planning for debates also includes the media coverage about the debate. If you want to make sure extracts are being replayed by the media and on social media, you have to prepare controversial statements. By the nature of how the media works, it is often contentious, emotional exchanges among the candidates that get picked up and repeated.

I recommend conducting mock debates at the time of day when the real debate will take place. I have, for example, spent entire debate preps teaching a client how to pivot away from attacks that we were sure would be coming. Ideally, allies of the candidate fill in and "play" the opponent candidates. A good example of that is the 2020 US presidential debates between challenger Joe Biden and incumbent

Donald Trump. The latter was well known for his aggressive debate style and so Biden could prepare accordingly. Attorney Bob Baur, who apparently played Donald Trump in Joe Biden's mock debates, was probably behaving in that same manner.[118] I assume he was constantly interrupting Biden, ignoring debate rules, maybe even ridiculing his opponent. Most likely, Biden's advisers trained him to stay cool, ignore his opponent despite any provocation, and speak directly to the audience.

Opposition candidates in particular should invest time in debate preparation because debates are a great opportunity for challengers. Incumbents are usually out of practice debating. It is also much harder to get them to study and rehearse for debates. In addition to running a campaign, incumbents also run a country, state, or city. They are faced with various crises and emergencies on a daily basis, so there is always a valid, sound reason to delay debate preparation. Incumbents also usually think that they know the issues already since they are dealing with them on a daily basis. They are also not used to people standing next to them disagreeing with everything they say. A challenger should therefore take maximum advantage of that opportunity. A great example of this was the first debate between challenger Mitt Romney against incumbent president Barack Obama. It was the best ninety minutes Romney had as a candidate. He was on the offense and looked like he was enjoying every one of those ninety minutes. Barack Obama, on the other hand, looked tired and almost annoyed that he had to go through this. You probably won't be surprised to learn that Romney did ten mock debates prior to the actual event.[119]

HOW MEDIOCRE SPEAKERS DELIVER GREAT SPEECHES

Call me a wonk, but I like to read politicians' speeches. In a US presidential election, there are a few signature speeches: to announce the candidacy, to accept the nomination after winning the primary, and to declare victory in the case of winning the general election. Later on, and once in office, there is the State of the Union Address, when the president reports to Congress once a year about the state of the country. With the exception of the announcement speech, these speeches are often televised entirely and therefore have an important nationwide TV audience. In other countries, it is the speeches for New Year or the national holiday that are televised directly and represent similar opportunities to speak directly to the voters. If you are running for mayor or governor, chances are that you will not give such a high-profile speech. In these situations, candidates give what we call the stump speech—the regular speech a candidate gives several times a day on the campaign trail, which should essentially communicate the campaign message.

Some politicians are naturally gifted, outstanding public speakers and have built their entire careers around speeches. Barack Obama is a good example of that. His speech at the 2004 Democratic National Convention when he was a young senator catapulted him into the national limelight. His announcement speech jump-started his unlikely run for the presidency. After winning the nomination, he moved his acceptance speech outdoors to a football stadium in order to deliver it in front of tens of thousands of people. Even before becoming president, when he was still a candidate, Obama delivered a high-profile speech abroad in Berlin, Germany. It was an unusual thing to do for a candidate, but a stunning crowd of more than a hundred thousand people came out to listen what Obama had to say.

Then, there are mediocre speakers who sometimes deliver great speeches. An example I learned about years ago when I was at the Graduate School of Political Management is that of George H. W. Bush running for president in 1988. While he was probably not the most gifted public speaker, he delivered a great speech at the Republican National Convention when he was officially nominated as candidate. Before the start of the convention, Bush, then the incumbent vice president to Ronald Reagan, was trailing his opponent by seventeen points in the surveys.[120] In terms of strategic goals, Bush had a lot to accomplish with that convention speech: he had to take credit for the accomplishments of the Reagan administration but step out of his shadow and define himself as his own man. He had to convince the party base that he was conservative enough, reach out to independents, and most importantly, take on his opponent. Bush delivered an electrifying speech, which was the beginning of his comeback.[121] He spoke of himself as a quiet man "who hears the quiet people." He energized a party base that was eagerly waiting. "Many of you have asked, 'When will this campaign really begin?' I have come to this hall to tell you, and to tell America: tonight is the night."[122] With respect to drawing contrast with his opponent, Bush did it in a brilliant way. He didn't accuse his opponent of positions that the opponent would refuse to have taken. He chose issues such as abortion, the Pledge of Allegiance, or the death penalty, knowing that the majority of voters would disagree with his opponent's positions. A key line from the speech addressed the issue of taxes when Bush famously said, "Read my lips, no new taxes."[123]

If you are one of the less naturally gifted public speakers, it is advisable to get some professional training. Public speaking is something that can be learned like a foreign language, and the fear of it can be overcome. Especially if you are not a particularly good public speaker, then stick to shorter speeches. If a candidate cannot do better in an hour than in ten minutes, then he'd better speak for ten minutes. A simple yet sound piece of advice I once heard about speeches is the following: open strong, finish strong, and make people laugh at least twice in between. When I was practicing for my TEDx talk on winning elections in a changing world, I followed that rule. We invested much time thinking about the start and the end of the speech. During the rehearsal, I tested a joke, but while it didn't perform well, I was at least left with another spontaneous laugh during the actual speech.

One speech I hope you will never need is a concession speech. While losing an election is definitely painful, the playbook on how to concede is simple. The more the loser admits defeat and praises the winner, the better it will come across and the more people will say that you acted like a statesman. This is a better position in which to end a career or launch a comeback than to be seen as someone who cannot accept defeat. I know that this is easy to say but emotionally difficult to pull off in practice. I have worked for candidates who lost, and I have seen how it feels. Accepting a loss nonetheless comes across much better than trying to spin an obvious defeat into a victory. As a terrible example, I remember Armin Laschet, candidate for chancellor in Germany in 2021. On election eve, his party lost almost 8 percent and had the worst result since World War II, yet he proclaimed his intention to lead the next government. At that time, the CDU still had a slim chance to form a coalition government, but the way he claimed the chancellorship was out of step with the reality of the result.[124] The CDU landed on the opposition benches and Laschet was out of the picture. A great example of how to concede, on the other hand, was when John McCain lost the presidential election to Barack Obama in 2008. McCain emphasized the historic nature of Obama's election as the first African American elected to the White House. Then he went on to say this:

> I urge all Americans who supported me to join me in not just congratulating him, but offering our next president our goodwill and earnest effort to find ways to come together, to find the necessary compromises, to bridge our differences and help restore our prosperity, defend our security in a dangerous world, and leave our children and grandchildren a stronger, better country than we inherited. Whatever our differences, we are fellow Americans. And please believe me when I say no association has ever meant more to me than that.[125]

HOW TO ASSEMBLE A TOP-NOTCH CAMPAIGN TEAM

Election campaigns are chaotic, ad hoc operations. At the beginning of a campaign, campaign teams oftentimes operate with limited resources and are hastily put together. Consultants and staffers who had not known each other previously come together. They may have different backgrounds, sometimes even different agendas, but often share big egos. Once a campaign seems to be on the road to success, it grows rapidly, which does not make the management easier. In high-profile nationwide campaigns, there are oftentimes multiple structures, multiple media advisers, multiple pollsters, and multiple strategic decision-making centers. What they normally share is that the top candidate is part of each one of them. In that sense, campaigns are unique because everything is geared toward the top candidate. The brain of the candidate is where all the threads come together and there is usually a competition for the candidate's attention among the senior people. Beyond the official campaign team, candidates are usually bombarded with advice from friends, family, donors, and allies.

While this is the very nature of campaigns, candidates deal with it differently. The top candidates play a key role in establishing discipline and one that only they can fulfill. There are candidates who absorb advice like a sponge. They talk to their campaign staff in the morning, businessmen and party mates in the afternoon, and friends and family members in the evening. By the time they go to bed, they are so confused that they do not know what to do anymore. The first consequence of this behavior by the top candidate is usually that decision-making is delayed. Endless discussions and turning in circles become the normal way of conducting things. The second consequence is that decisions are often changed. Agreements that take weeks and months to be reached can be undone, overthrown, and changed the next day. The problem is also that while these candidates listen to plenty of people volunteering advice, they do not trust anyone entirely. The asking for advice is often without real, lasting impact. These campaigns usually end up in complete chaos. When I decided to go out on my own and become a political consultant seventeen years ago, one of my first clients abroad was the type that would listen to everyone. It was a local campaign where everything could easily be managed. Being the young man that I was at the time, I decided to surround my client all the time. I would try to be at his house before he woke up and would only leave his house once he went to bed. While the candidate in question ended up winning the election, that approach is not feasible for more sophisticated nationwide campaigns. A leader who signals to his team that there is a back door through which decisions can be undermined and undone can be sure that advisers and staffers will use it. If a candidate tolerates turf wars, people will slug them out for sure. As a result, I have seen campaign teams that literally had more interest in fighting and bad-mouthing each other than in winning the election. The friend of a client recently told me, "Louis, our campaign is in complete chaos." In such a situation, it is best to try and focus on the common enemy. Complete chaos where everyone is fighting the other side is better than complete chaos fighting each other. It's unfortunately not always possible. There are candidates whose very style of leadership is to pit various factions against each other. They think that the result will be better if various brains compete. I have been in a campaign where several consultants were negotiating the seconds of the television ad. The outcome of that process will definitely not be a coherent message but a sure way to lose an election. A typical mistake for party leaders is also to include everyone in the decision-making or even to conduct internal surveys about strategic questions, thinking that the decision will then be more legitimate and broadly supported by the rank and file. It never works. Electoral success will silence internal critics much more effectively than any amount of internal party democracy.

There is a myth that all feedback is worth listening to. As a matter of fact, no! As consultant Alan Weiss correctly says, unsolicited feedback is almost always for the one giving and not the one receiving it.[126] People may not be competent to give feedback or may have their own agenda in doing so. It's crucially important for candidates to carefully vet and choose their inner circle. Once chosen, though, candidates have to empower their teams and ask for cooperation and discipline. Effective campaigns are like a guerrilla attack. Among other things, this means that decision-making is quick, that you're on the offense and can surprise your opponent, and that your team is cohesive and fights as one. In other words: discipline is a key factor for electoral success. As different as they may be politically, Barack Obama and George W. Bush are both great examples of how to establish and maintain internal order. Even in presidential elections with hundreds of staff, only about a handful of people were involved in key decisions.

A good campaign manager should foremost have management skills. Effective managers have the trust of the candidate and ideally also have some political know-how (or at least be realistic about the lack thereof). When I start to work with a campaign, I have a simple test to assess the organizational structure of the campaign. I ask who the campaign manager is. It happens quite often that I get several different answers, which I take as an indication that the campaign has a management problem. I have also been in campaigns where a handful of people thought they were the manager. Other times, there is someone officially called campaign manager, but that person has no real power and another, unofficial person acts as the real campaign manager. To begin with, a campaign manager should have at least some discretionary decision-making power regarding budget and staff. If one is not allowed to decide on a certain amount of money oneself and cannot hire and fire staff for midlevel positions, then that person is not the campaign manager. In that case, the person labeled campaign manager is de facto the executive assistant of the real campaign manager, who is probably a family member of the candidate. This does not necessarily have to be a problem. I have been in campaigns where the spouse or a sibling of the candidate was de facto running the operation. When they were politically savvy themselves, these turned out to be some of the most disciplined campaigns I have ever worked for. In some countries, it is common to appoint other politicians as campaign managers. I am, however, highly skeptical of that as they will always have their own agenda.

In addition to the campaign manager, there will likely be media people (press, advertising, social media), a pollster, a scheduler or executive assistant, a finance person, political operatives, and consultants. When you put together your team, it is also important to remember that the barriers to enter our industry are low. As a result, there are, unfortunately, crooks who promise candidates the sky and the moon—for example, votes in exchange for patronage or droves of online supporters. We all want our clients to be in the best possible position, but we must remember a simple rule: if what a consultant, operative, advertiser, or social media expert promises sounds too good to be true, it probably isn't true. Here is a checklist of questions to ask when putting together a team:

- What campaigns have you worked on that are similar to mine? What were your lessons learned? And what was your specific contribution? (Listen carefully to the answer to the last question, because as the saying goes, success has many fathers, failure is an orphan.)
- How do you think my campaign will be different from those that you have just mentioned? (While we always wish for the same outcome, electoral success, each campaign is different. Beware of consultants and agencies who have a claim to fame and then go on copying and pasting that formula for any other

client. These people soon become a one-trick pony and are occasionally pretty bad at what they are supposed to be good at.)

- Can you provide any references from other candidates whom I may call? (Then I encourage you to make those calls.)
- How many other clients or campaigns do you handle at the same time? (Make sure you get the attention you deserve. One of the main reasons why great people screw up is because we take on too much.)
- Whom will I deal with on a daily basis? (I think it's a gentleman agreement that the person who makes a pitch is also the person who is heading the account and is involved on a regular basis.)
- Have you ever left a candidate during a campaign? (I find it unprofessional to leave a candidate during the heat of a campaign for minor reasons. Unless there is a major strategic disagreement or something like an abuse, a campaign operative should not do it. At least, the hurdle should be high. I have had a candidate yell at me during a call late at night. You get over it. Campaigns are intense, and the candidate can be under enormous pressure.)
- Have you ever lost a campaign? What have you learned from it? (Beware of magicians who supposedly have never lost a campaign. They may be lying to you or be too risk-averse when accepting clients. While I learned more from winning than from losing campaigns, I also picked up painful but important lessons from my losses.)
- How do you think political campaigns are different from product campaigns? (Beware of commercial advertisers who claim that there is no difference and that they will make you a brand. Mostly, they will make you look like a fool. Political campaigns may use some of the same tools as campaigns for products, but the content, the timing, and the dynamics of election campaigns are different from campaigns for products.)

LET US TALK ABOUT MONEY

Next, let us talk about money. Few other topics are as intriguing to people. When I speak to politicians or give interviews to journalists, I notice that they often want to hear an all-or-nothing answer. On the one hand, some want to hear that money is everything in a campaign and can create wonders at the polls. In Switzerland, there is a famous saying that with a million Swiss francs, you can transform a bag of potatoes into a federal councillor (the name for our government members). In the US, there is another quote by former Speaker of the House of Representatives Thomas Phillip "Tip" O'Neill that money "is the mother's milk of politics."[127]

Others like to hear the opposite, namely that money does not matter all that much in campaigns. The green parties are often mentioned as an example of parties who win without much money. They often do have limited campaign funds but nevertheless have celebrated impressive successes in several European countries. It is also often new parties, who ride a wave of free media, who bring home electoral success with a limited amount of money. On the other hand, I have mentioned that Michael Bloomberg, the former mayor of New York, spent more than $1 billion on his bid for the Democratic presidential nomination in 2020. It was a truly stunning and record-breaking amount for a primary campaign that only lasted a few months, yet he was far off from winning the nomination.[128] To make things worse, I doubt you would even remember any ad or message from his campaign by now. Another example is Jaime Harrison, the Democrat who ran for Senate in South Carolina, challenging incumbent Lindsey Graham. Harris broke the quarterly fundraising record for a Senate candidate in the US. During the last quarter of the campaign, he raised a stunning $57 million.[129] On election night, he lost 44 percent to 55 percent.[130] I could go on and on with examples to tell you that money is not a guarantee of success. As a matter of fact, too much money can even become a liability for a campaign as it possibly undermines message and decision-making discipline. If there are unlimited resources, a campaign team is not forced to make strategic decisions. They can afford to air as many ads with as many messages as they want, but without message discipline, the appeal of the candidacy is diluted. This is admittedly not a problem that I face frequently, but I did experience it with a couple of my clients.

In my experience, the truth is somewhere in between these all-or-nothing positions. Money in itself does not communicate a message, nor can it create enthusiasm. It does not replace a solid and winning campaign plan and message. This being said, money is *one of the* important factors in a campaign. The key is to have *enough* money to implement your campaign plan and to communicate your message to your target audience. Now, how much money is enough? It is a question that many candidates never ask themselves. As a matter of fact, most candidates think about it in the exact opposite way: they think about how much they can possibly raise, then they think about how they will spend that amount. I learned that sound planning should follow the reverse order:

1. What is the goal?
2. How many votes does it take to reach that goal?
3. What is the plan I need to implement in order to realistically reach that goal?
4. What is the price tag for that plan?
5. How will we raise that amount of money?

The answer to the fourth question is the amount that is enough for your campaign; that is the amount you should try to raise.

While the present book is not about fundraising and therefore does not fully answer question five, I observe that the nature of fundraising is changing. In the old days, candidates would court the rich. There would be exclusive events, say US$1,000 per plate, where you can get to know the candidate and take a picture together. The trend I observe now is that fundraising is moving toward a model with a large number of small donors. Joe Biden, for example, literally had millions of people who donated $20, $30, or $40.[131] These people are not invited to a dinner, and they do not expect to ever meet Joe Biden. The driving force here is not access or prestige; rather, it is emotion. If people are angry or worried, they want to do something. As a campaign, give them an opportunity to do something, namely, to donate money. When the US Supreme Court justice Ruth Bader Ginsburg died shortly before the last presidential election, it soon became clear that Donald Trump and Republicans would be able to fill the vacant seat and change the majority of the highest court of the land for decades to come. It deeply worried liberals across the country. It also turned out to be some of the best fundraising days for liberal candidates. You could also call this approach message-driven fundraising. The ingredients for this are the following: First, well, a message that is tremendously emotionally appealing. Second, one needs good data to target potential donors. And third, it takes a tremendous amount of work to repeatedly ask for money. The key is to ask the donor base again, and again, and again. In order to make such an effort sustainable, it also helps to present a clear plan for how you intend to reach your goals.

Because of the intriguing and emotional nature of the topic, money is also commonly used as an excuse. What I mean by this is that quite often candidates who lose an election blame the lack of money for their failure. Their rationale goes like this: "We lost because the other side had much more money than we did." Leftist parties and candidates are particularly good at this. The truth, however, is that if you knew that a lack of funds will be a challenge going into the race, then why did you not invest more time, attention, and resources into fundraising? I learned that as a rule of thumb, a fundraising disadvantage becomes a real problem if the ratio goes beyond one to two. If your opponent has more than double the amount of money than you have, you risk having a problem with visibility. If that is the situation, you have to raise more money. Politicians around the world often think that fundraising is more ingrained in the US culture and that it is therefore easier for American politicians to raise money than for themselves in their local context. This is not necessarily true. American candidates just invest much more time in fundraising than politicians elsewhere. Depending on the season and the race, it can take up half of their time.

LAST PIECE OF ADVICE

My last piece of advice for this chapter is not to lose your cool when the race tightens toward the end of the campaign. I am not advocating to lean back or to be complacent. If you are approaching election day and you are in a free fall, then you need drastic action. And generally speaking, I almost always prefer to be on the offense than on the defense in such moments. This said, it is quite common that races tighten when election day approaches; remember that surveys showing a tightening race will also get more media attention than those indicating that the race is over. Be aware of it when it happens, be on top of things, but do not panic.

7

WHEN EVERYTHING YOU KNOW HITS THE FAN AND THE FAN BREAKS—A CRASH COURSE IN CRISIS MANAGEMENT

Jim Messina, the campaign manager for Barack Obama's reelection campaign in 2012, used to say that his favorite political philosopher is Mike Tyson.[132] If you are running for office in a high-profile, competitive race, chances are that you will be the target of attacks. That should be the working hypothesis, and you'd better prepare accordingly so as to be ready to answer them. Once your opponent starts to hit you, you can even take it as a compliment because it means that others give you a chance to win. In German there's a saying "*tote Hunde tritt man nicht*," which translated word for word means that nobody beats a dead dog. It signifies that your opponents will only attack you if they think that you are a threat to them. I have personally worked for clients who were accused of corruption, gambling, womanizing, drug abuse, being a turncoat, incurring government debts, excessive drinking, land grabbing, overpriced projects, doubtful alliances, and having ghost employees. Yet other clients of mine were accused of not hailing from the area, not being a citizen, having been in office for too long, or being too old, too radical, or too religious. In this chapter, I want to give you some practical advice based on my experiences on how to deal with such a crisis situation. I explain why new candidates are particularly vulnerable to attacks and detail the five basic strategic options on how to deal with them.

In the US, attacks are launched explicitly. "Everybody loves a fight" is a common saying. The relentless airing of paid TV commercials is the heart of most US election campaigns, and most of those ads are attack ads hitting the opponent. The situation is different in other countries, where, depending on the political culture, things are said more implicitly. Regardless of the tone and whether attacks are launched directly by your opponent or indirectly via the media, they will come, and they will be brutal.

WHY NEW CANDIDATES ARE PARTICULARLY VULNERABLE TO ATTACKS

As a challenger you are particularly vulnerable to attacks and allegations because your image is likely not yet firmly defined in people's minds. In other words, if you are new on the (national) political scene, voters have limited information about you, and as a result, an attack might represent an important portion of the information voters have about you. Whether or not they're true, the allegations could stick and come to define you in the eyes of the citizens you want on your side. Incumbents and politicians with established names are in a much more comfortable situation. Voters usually have plenty of information about them as they have seen them in the news for years. Allegations that have been out there about an incumbent are already factored in by voters in their overall assessment of the politician in question. Repeating the same or a similar allegation does not provide new information, and if an accusation is truly new, it represents only a small fraction of the information voters have about the incumbent. I have also seen many times in focus groups that if voters have known someone for a while, they become suspicious about the timing of attacks shortly before an election ("I have seen the governor and his work for three and a half years, why is that allegation only being spread now?").

The German election in 2021 provides a good illustration of the vulnerability of a young or new candidacy. The Green Party nominated Annalena Baerbock, forty years old, as their top candidate for chancellor. Baerbock had previously served as a member of the German parliament and the coleader of the Green Party. At the beginning, the media reported very positively about her candidacy. After she was designated the top candidate, journalists even applauded at the end of a televised interview with her.[133] As is often the case, the honeymoon with the media soon came to an end when it was reported that Baerbock had embellished her professional résumé. Then it became public that she had forgotten to report additional income as is mandatory for members of the German parliament. Soon thereafter, it was also reported that Baerbock had plagiarized several times in a book she had published at the beginning of the election year. Over time, experts found dozens of paragraphs that were copied and pasted from other sources without proper referencing. It was no coincidence that all these stories broke at a time when the Green Party was doing exceptionally well in the surveys. At one moment, it even looked possible that it could become the biggest party of Germany, and in that case, Baerbock would have become chancellor.

A consequence of this success in the surveys was that voters, pundits, and analysts suddenly became particularly interested in Baerbock. As there appeared to be a possibility of Baerbock becoming chancellor, she rapidly became a target. In any previous election when the Greens were not polling well, chances are that no one would have looked so closely at her résumé, her income declarations, and her book. Unfortunately for her, the three allegations were similar in nature. She could probably have dismissed a single one of them, but the three together were difficult to ignore, as they painted a picture of someone who easily glossed over inconvenient details to further her own career. As a result of the allegations, voters increasingly started to question her character and her readiness to lead Germany. Until the end of the campaign, Baerbock was unable to recover fully from the attacks. On election day, the Greens increased their vote share and got almost 15 percent of the vote. It was a good result, but it was more than ten points away from becoming the biggest party.

What could Baerbock and her team have done differently? The challenge in crisis management is that decisions on how to respond to an accusation have to be made rapidly after it becomes public. In order to make the right decisions, though, you have to know (all) the facts. In that sense, crisis management is much like walking in a labyrinth. If you take a wrong turn at the beginning, everything that follows will be wrong as well. Lesson number one in crisis communication, therefore, is this: immediately get all the facts. I learned this many years ago at the Graduate School of Political Management in Washington, DC, and have tried to apply it ever since. If you are the candidate at the center of the attack, you have a good chance of knowing the facts, but even then, there is no guarantee. The incident leading to the accusation might have happened years or even decades ago. What is culturally accepted behavior and language may have changed, and records may have disappeared. Prove to me immediately and on the spot that you never robbed a bank twenty years ago. You may reply to me that that is a ridiculous accusation, but you may well be faced with ridiculous accusations during the campaign. For the advisers, the challenge is even bigger because they surely do not know the facts and have to trust the candidate's recollection of information.

FIVE STRATEGIC OPTIONS TO DEAL WITH ATTACKS

Once an attack is launched against you, these are the five strategic options to deal with it:

- Ignore it
- Ridicule it
- Own it
- Take legal action
- Deny it (and hit back)

Ignore It

In many countries, we now, by and large, have a twenty-four-hour news cycle and various media outlets compete for attention. In such an environment, it has become difficult to simply ignore and sit out a major allegation. That strategy might work if you are far ahead in the surveys and it is already close to election day. By responding, you will likely make the story bigger, so ignoring it can be promising if you are the clear front-runner and the finish line is in sight. To ignore an attack might also work when there is a good chance that voters themselves do not believe the allegation. In my experience, this is often the case when candidates are attacked for things that relate to their personal lives. Just because an attack is out there does not mean that voters believe it. In that sense, let it be clear that not every tweet and Facebook post is a crisis and in need of a reply. Focus groups are a useful tool to find out whether voters who are not political insiders believe an allegation. I have been in situations where the research showed that voters were dismissing allegations that were thrown at my candidate. For example, I worked for a candidate who was attacked with many things, yet voters in the focus groups either did not believe it or even defended the candidate. At some point, I gained the impression in our focus groups that it had become emotional for voters—they had made up their minds and wanted to vote for my candidate. As a result, they stopped listening to the various attacks. So, in such a situation, why make the story bigger by responding? The candidate ignored all attacks and won a big victory. Or, as Michelle Obama used to say, "When they go low, we go high."[134]

Ridicule It

A great example of ridiculing attacks comes from Ukrainian president Volodymyr Zelensky. As mentioned earlier, Zelensky was a famous comedian, and his run for the presidency was his first election campaign ever. When he was rising in the polls and became a threat, his opponents started to hit him with what he called fake scandals. As a reaction, Zelensky asked his supporters to create more fake accusations and made a competition out of it. He asked his followers to send in the most absurd charges. During the course of this exercise, Zelensky became a woman, the illegitimate daughter of a political opponent, or the lover of German chancellor Angela Merkel. Like a drawing, Zelensky then chose the winning allegation, which portrayed him as a descendant of the Rothschild banking family. As a former comedian, he was uniquely well positioned for such a strategy. The beauty of this approach is also that with this reaction, he was effectively dealing with and dismissing all allegations against him in one. I have used that same strategy for a client of mine who was running for congress. Once she was seen to be rising in the polls, her opponents started to attack her. Among other things, she was accused of not being a natural-born citizen, which was required by law to run in that country. It so happened that another candidate who was running for president at the same time was also accused of not being a natural-born citizen. We used this coincidence to ridicule the attack. "Wow, I'm honored they throw the same things at me as at a presidential candidate," my client said and won a stunning upset.

Own It

If the accusations are true, the best strategy (solely with respect to communication, not legally speaking) is to admit mistakes and to accept responsibility. When running for president, George W. Bush was confronted with an allegation that he had once been arrested for driving a car under the influence of alcohol. The story broke a few days before election day. Bush stood in front of the cameras and admitted that the incident had happened, saying that he was not proud of it but had learned his lesson.[135] If that is the route you decide to take, time is of the essence. The faster you admit a mistake, and the more wholeheartedly, the more people are willing to forgive. People generally find confessions refreshing and are inclined to forgive. If you do admit to something, this is not the time to blame others (which you can still do later on as time goes by) but rather to promise concrete action in order to put the crisis to rest.

Take Legal Action

Depending on the situation, it can be the right strategy to take legal action against those spreading the accusation. After all, I can't think of any group of people that has to absorb more insults and abuses of privacy rights than those in politics. In some countries, the law is actually favorable to pursue such a strategy, yet politicians are often reluctant to do it. There are several reasons for this: legal processes can be very long, and by the time you clear your name, you are long dead politically. By pursuing the legal route, you might also make the story bigger and keep it alive in the news. You might look overly sensitive and fuel speculations. It is also important to understand that a legal strategy is, in fact, decidedly different from a communication strategy. Lawyers usually want to say as little as possible, and depending on the case, that might be the smart thing to do, but in terms of communication, "no comment" is difficult to maintain over time.

Deny It (And Hit Back)

Yet another possible strategy is to deny an allegation. You should only opt for this strategy if the allegation really is untrue. I would highly recommend not to take this route if there is a risk that the denial can be proven wrong, because in that case, it will create much more damage. You'd better be sure before making that decision because there is hardly any room to walk back. If a media outlet is breaking a story of a major scandal, it is highly likely that they know more about the allegation than what they publish in the first piece (or that they will soon find out more once the story is published). It is therefore important not to deny an allegation out of reflex. In many cases, an accused person becomes defensive and instinctively denies the accusation. While this is natural and understandable, it often makes things worse. Sometimes, it's the instant lying that triggers the real and even bigger (legal) problem. A prominent example is former French minister Jérôme Cahuzac, who was accused of having an undeclared bank account in Switzerland. "Looking at me face-to-face, do you have a secret bank account in Switzerland?" a journalist asked. Cahuzac passionately denied it.[136] Only a bit later, he was forced to admit that he indeed had an account in Switzerland. It was the end of his political career, and he was sentenced to prison.[137]

If you can support your denial with specific proof from a credible source, that's tremendously helpful. It is also important to keep a denial short since extended explanations might turn the electorate off or make people suspicious. We all know this from daily private life: if people feel the need to explain themselves about something extensively, it usually creates more doubts in our minds about what they have to hide. In that sense, a denial should be short and clear. These denials are often coupled with counterattacks, and ideally you go back to the original campaign message when doing that: "They attack me for inappropriate behavior thirty years ago because they do not want to talk about their terrible government record during the pandemic."

As mentioned at the beginning of the chapter, it is important not to underestimate attacks, because a challenger is particularly vulnerable to them. Among political consultants, we use the term "being swift boated" to describe the phenomenon of a candidate being destroyed by attacks and negative ads. The term refers to the presidential campaign of John Kerry when he challenged incumbent President George W. Bush in 2004. Kerry made his military service during the Vietnam War a central piece of his campaign message and qualification to become president. Kerry had served as a commanding officer on a swift boat and had earned several military awards for it. During the election campaign, however, some war veterans started to attack Kerry's credentials. A group called "Swift Boat Veterans for Truth" came together and started to air TV ads. In those ads, they accused Kerry of lying about his war credentials. Kerry had only served so that he could later exploit it for political purposes back home, they alleged. The group of veterans also claimed that Kerry had betrayed them by later opposing the war and joining the antiwar movement. At the beginning, the group invested a moderate amount of a couple of hundred thousand dollars to buy TV ads in three selected states. The first commercial—called "Any Questions?"—was sixty seconds long and started with footage from a campaign rally where John Kerry's own vice presidential candidate, John Edwards, said, "If you have any questions about what John Kerry is made of, just spend three minutes with the men who served with him." Then the ad changed in tone and the Swift Boat Veterans for Truth were featured. "Here's what these men say," the voiceover said. "John Kerry has not been honest about what happened in Vietnam." "John Kerry is lying about his record." "John Kerry is lying about his first Purple Heart, because I treated him for that injury." "John Kerry lied about his Bronze Star. I know, I was there, I saw what happened." "John Kerry betrayed the men and women he served with." "He lied before the Senate."[138] It was brutal. Soon after the ads started airing, Kerry's advisers noticed an impact in their internal polling. It was not a dramatic shift in the numbers at first, but it was noticeable. The team started to discuss how to best respond. As is typical for such a situation, there were those who thought that the drop in the numbers was caused by something else. Other advisers were arguing that responding to it would make the story bigger. Yet some concluded that the ad would only impact Republicans and not swing voters. Time passed and the fire grew bigger. Ultimately, the Swift Boat Veterans for Truth created a series of ads and raised close to $30 million.[139] In my assessment, it was a key reason why Kerry lost the election. At the time, there were several media investigations that challenged the allegations of the Swift Boat Veterans for Truth, which could have been used in a more forceful rebuttal. There were also groups of other veterans supporting Kerry and his version of what happened during the war. John Kerry himself apparently wanted to respond more vigorously, and in hindsight, I think it would clearly have been better.[140]

A candidate that would definitely never let himself be swift boated is Donald Trump. Whether you like or dislike him, there is one thing every politician can learn from him—if you do not stand up for yourself, you lose your biggest advocate. Remember during the 2016 campaign when the *Access Hollywood* tape became public a few weeks before the election? In the tape, made public by the *Washington Post*, Trump was seen and heard talking about harassing women. As a celebrity, he could get away with "grabbing them by the pussy," Trump bragged.[141] The media jumped at the story, and there was a huge outcry. I remember exactly where I was on the weekend when the story broke: in a radio studio, discussing the scandal. There were even talks about this being the end of Trump's candidacy. As we now know, it was not the end. While it definitely did not help his favorability ratings, he survived the scandal. I have spent a lot of time thinking about the reason for Trump surviving this, and I think that the first part of the explanation is that his wife, Melania Trump, and his running mate,

Mike Pence, stuck by him during the crisis. The fact that Trump was the first presidential candidate in US history to have a female campaign manager, Kellyanne Conway, was also helpful in countering the accusation that Trump was antiwomen. In addition to that, it was key that he had never defined himself as particularly feminist. He had defined himself as an outsider who would shake up Washington, DC, and a successful businessman who would make America great again. Voters did not like what they saw and heard in the *Access Hollywood* tape, but it did not contradict how Trump had defined himself. As a result, he was able to get away with it.

Put differently, this means that an allegation is particularly dangerous if it contradicts the self-definition of the candidate in question. If you have defined yourself as the one who will clean up government, and all of a sudden there are serious corruption allegations against you, that is potentially dangerous. If you have run on a message of economic recovery, and all of a sudden there are allegations of business failures, that could be potentially harmful for your ratings.

WHAT'S BEHIND MOST ATTACKS: OPPOSITION RESEARCH

The basis for most attacks, whether aired in TV commercials or published via the media, is opposition research. "Oppo," as it is called in campaign jargon, is the systematic gathering of information about the opponent. Opposition researchers look, for example, at tax returns, business records, campaign donations, or voting behavior. They search online and spend days and weeks in libraries and government archives or talking to former employees, former staff, and ex-spouses. The key here is first that the searching is done systematically. If a piece of information cannot be documented and validated, it is useless for a professional opposition researcher. Second, the goal is to look for patterns in the data. Ideally, it becomes possible to portray a candidate as someone who repeatedly voted for higher taxes, changed positions to fit changing political circumstances, or said something different in public than in private.

A good illustration is the case of Hillary Clinton, who ran for president against Donald Trump in 2016. During the campaign, it was said numerous times that Clinton was not a particularly appealing candidate. What many forget is that it had not always been that way. Clinton had served as secretary of state in the first Obama administration and was quite popular at that time. When Clinton stepped down from that position in order to prepare for her second run for the presidency, her approval rating was at a net positive: 64 percent of voters had a favorable opinion of her while 31 percent saw her unfavorably.[142] It is reasonable to expect her ratings to worsen during a highly politicized election campaign, but what was about to hit her was more than that.

A key event was the publication of a book named *Clinton Cash: The Untold Story of How and Why Foreign Governments and Businesses Helped Make Bill and Hillary Rich*. It was written by political consultant and author Peter Schweizer and published by HarperCollins, a major US publisher. The main allegation of the book is that former president Bill Clinton, through his charity, the Clinton Foundation, and Hillary Clinton, secretary of state at that time, worked in tandem to raise money. According to the book, foreign leaders who needed favors from the State Department donated generously to the Clinton Foundation.[143] The book had a substantial impact because its main allegation as well as many examples were picked up by mainstream reporters. In fact, advance copies of the book were provided to media outlets, including the *New York Times* and the *Washington Post*. That was a distinctively different approach from the one that was used against Hillary's husband, Bill Clinton, in the 1990s. Republicans were unable to bring him down because they were mainly talking to themselves inside their own Republican bubble. At that time, Republicans thought they were winning, when in fact they had lost mainstream voters and the mainstream media. *Clinton Cash*, on the other hand, offered precious research to journalists, who, always pressed for time, could simply pick it up and build on it. From a craft point of view, it was opposition research at its best. Without going into detail here, Clinton faced several additional challenges and allegations. For example, it became public that as secretary of state, she had used a private server for her emails, and by doing that she put classified information at risk of leaking. This all did serious damage to Clinton's approval rating. According to the exit polls on election day, 55 percent of the voters had an unfavorable view of Hillary Clinton while 43 percent had a favorable one.[144] Within a short period of time, she had turned from a reasonably popular political leader into the second most disliked presidential candidate in US history.

If you compare the attacks against Trump to those against Clinton, I think there is a crucial difference. The allegations against Clinton directly undermined her own message and the way she had defined herself. Experience and qualification to serve as president were key elements of Clinton's message, and the allegations against her (putting secret information at risk by using a private server, aggressive fundraising) directly went against that message. It is a key factor explaining why she, unlike Trump, was unable to politically survive the attacks against her. If you look at the examples above, the allegations against Hillary Clinton and John Kerry are things that the respective campaigns had to reasonably expect. Yet despite being high-profile, professional campaigns with plenty of experts and staff, they responded inadequately. Many campaign teams are great at seeing and realizing the weaknesses of the opponent (which is also important) but fail to see their own. It happens to me regularly that I exchange notes with politicians, and when we first talk about other candidates and campaigns, we agree on many things. It's only once we start to talk about their own case that we evaluate things differently, and I often think that they are totally in a bubble. I therefore strongly suggest that you test both—attacks, and possible rebuttals—in your internal research. In high-profile campaigns it has become the gold standard to produce and test attack ads against yourself to be fully prepared for what is about to hit you.

ALWAYS BE READY FOR A SURPRISE

While a candidate can and absolutely should have a long-term strategy for a campaign, one also always has to be ready for any kind of surprise. There might be external events that can turn everything upside down. Paul Wellstone, incumbent senator from Minnesota, was running for reelection when, eleven days before the election, his plane crashed and Wellstone died. Former vice president Walter Mondale replaced him as the Democratic candidate, which meant that the Republican candidate and challenger, Norm Coleman, faced a new opponent overnight. Another case is the Senate election in Missouri in the year 2000. Democratic candidate Mel Carnahan, who had served two terms as governor, challenged the incumbent senator, John Ashcroft. Three weeks before the election, Carnahan also died in a plane crash. In that case, the election pushed through with Carnahan's name on the ballot and the late Carnahan won on election day.

Another case relates to the Madrid train bombings that rocked Spain three days before the 2004 general election. One hundred and ninety-three people died in the explosions and two thousand were injured. The case is of particular interest because instead of uniting Spain, which could have been one outcome, the incident was immediately followed by a controversy on how the attack was handled by the incumbent government of José María Aznar. Leaders from Aznar's People's Party, *Partido Popular* (PP), claimed that the Basque separatist movement was responsible for the bombings. Others suspected that the attack was carried out by Islamic terrorists and that it had something to do with Aznar's decision for Spain to participate in the war in

Iraq, an undertaking that was highly controversial among the population. Following the attacks, nationwide demonstrations and protests demanded that the government tell the truth about the attacks. As a result, Aznar surprisingly lost the election to the opposition.[145]

The COVID-19 virus is the latest example of how dramatically things can change more or less overnight. At the beginning of the pandemic, the voting had to be delayed in some instances, such as, for example, in the French local elections. In other cases, it dramatically changed the context in which election campaigns took place. In the US, for example, Donald Trump was planning to run for reelection touting economic growth numbers, but all of a sudden, the pandemic became the number one issue. At first, he probably thought that he could sit the virus out and get back to the economy. As the number of cases continued to increase, this strategy became increasingly difficult. Instead of a referendum on the economy, the election became a referendum on Donald Trump's crisis management. While voters knew that Trump had not created the virus, they became increasingly skeptical of his handling of it. The pandemic soon also had dramatic economic consequences as people were losing their jobs and many applied for unemployment benefits. As the election season intensified, the discrepancy between the Republican discourse and what voters were seeing on television and experiencing in their daily lives became more and more pronounced. At the Republican National Convention, for example, the pandemic was barely mentioned. While this was in sync with Trump's base, it must have been a disconnect with swing voters and independents who were otherwise watching news about the record number of new cases, deaths, lockdown, and economic downturn.

I am sometimes asked how often and under what circumstances a campaign should change the message. As a matter of fact, you should not have to change the message. You may have to adapt to current events and, depending on the situation, emphasize a different aspect of it, but if you feel the urge to change it fundamentally, it is a sign that your campaign is in trouble. You should only change your message if the fundamental assumptions on which it was based have changed. The case of Donald Trump's reelection campaign and COVID-19 is a good example of such a situation. The strategic premises on which his reelection campaign was based had changed within a few weeks. In particular, I think that the very last moment he could have changed his message was when he contracted COVID-19 himself and was released from the hospital. He did not, and the rest is history.

The COVID-19 virus is, in that sense, a particularly interesting phenomenon. All leaders were forced to deal with the same virus but did so by pursuing different strategies. Some leaders even benefited from the crisis in the polls. At the beginning of the crisis, the approval rating of German chancellor Angela Merkel, for example, rose to levels she had not seen in many years. The same was true for Canadian prime minister Justin Trudeau and French president Emmanuel Macron. If handled properly, a crisis can be an opportunity for a political leader to show mettle and proactivity. During a crisis, viewer- and readership of the news usually shoot up and people are more informed about what their leaders are doing. While the practice of crisis management is extremely challenging, the theory and the manual are quite straightforward: during a time of crisis, a president, prime minister, governor, or mayor has to act quickly. They should be on top of things, release emergency funds, and give the experts and frontliners everything they need. A leader should hit the right tone in his crisis communication. A crisis is also an opportunity for a political leader to show that he stands above partisanship. Rudy Giuliani was never more popular as mayor of New York than right after the terrorist attacks of 9/11. Gerhard Schröder won a surprising reelection in 2002 after staging himself as crisis manager fighting the flooding of the Elbe, an episode I write more about in chapter 9. And who knows if Barack Obama would have gotten reelected so convincingly had he not been seen as a crisis manager who put politics aside when Hurricane Sandy hit the East Coast a few days before the election?

LAST PIECE OF ADVICE

The best and easiest way to prepare for any possible allegation is to spread more good news about yourself and what you are doing for voters. The more positive information voters have about you, your credentials, and your accomplishments, the better prepared you are to weather the storm of a potential crisis. I realized this once I conducted focus groups for a client in a developing country; if voters saw plenty of projects from a leader, they concluded that there could hardly be much corruption. If they did not see projects, the allegation of corruption seemed credible to them. Alan Weiss, a business consultant, famously said that "if you don't blow your own horn, there is no music."[146] It is also true for electoral politics, and I therefore advise you to blow your own horn daily. Never assume that voters know what you have done for them. It is your job to tell them, and if you do not, no one else will.

8

HOW CHALLENGERS TURN INTO STATESMEN AND RUN FOR REELECTION

I once consulted with a candidate for governor. He was a native son of the province he was looking to lead and truly was made for the job. His main challenge was the intraparty fight for the nomination, but even the general election could not be taken for granted. After an intense campaign, he was elected. We spoke on the phone a few weeks after he had been sworn in. "It is really cool to govern," he said. "Everywhere you go, you sit on top of the table and are the boss. Everyone waits for your decision. And even if others first disagree, in the end, things are done the way you want." His description of governing is pretty accurate, but it reflects only half of the story. The transition from an opposition leader to a statesman has its own challenges.

Whoever you beat on election day will soon start to criticize every step you make. In many political systems, in fact, the opposition does little other than speak against the incumbent government. Your own party and allies will put pressure on you in order to get what they want. By the time you are serving, you are no longer the new kid in town. As a consequence, the media's very job is now to critique what you are doing as an elected official.

The first issue I want to address in this chapter is how to shift from being a candidate to being the official that holds the office. As soon as candidates get elected, aside from doing the job for which they were elected, they begin looking ahead to their next campaign. This future goal is the second topic I tackle in this chapter, since holding office and doing what it takes to remain in office go hand in hand. In other words, the transition from challenger to statesman is an important part of your reelection effort. In this chapter, I discuss how to make that transition smoothly and how to prepare for a possibly easy reelection. An election with an incumbent is a referendum on the incumbent. Next time, the incumbent will be you and you will want to begin in a position of strength. In that sense, the most effective election campaign of an incumbent does not look like an election campaign. It doesn't say "vote for Jennifer Smith" but communicates on a regular basis what Jennifer Smith is doing for voters in order to strengthen her job approval rating.

FROM CANDIDATE TO LEADER

The first step to winning reelection is to thank everyone who has helped you get elected in the first place. Ideally, you call them personally and make them feel that their contribution was the deciding factor for your election. I have experienced that myself several times—clients who told me how crucial I was to their success. I know that winning elections is always a team effort and there is rarely one single piece or contribution that makes or breaks a campaign. It nevertheless feels very nice when a president-elect writes you how instrumental you were in his campaign. As I mentioned earlier, if you want to go into public office, then welcome to the relationship business. Politics is about people. Beyond saying thank you, and if you want to be effective while in office, you will need to build relationships with the following people:

- People on the other side and in other parties
- Journalists
- People you dislike within your own ranks
- Various leaders in the legislative branch of government who will help you pass meaningful legislation if you are in an executive position

Building relationships is something that cannot be delegated. You have to do it yourself, and after winning an election, you can and should do that from a position of strength. It is a natural human feeling to want to gloat or think of vengeance right after winning. I strongly advise against it. Successful politicians don't burn bridges, they don't pick unnecessary fights, and they don't let people feel that they hold grudges. On the contrary, after you win an election is a great time to reach out to enemies. Try not to take things all too personally. Make it clear to both individuals and groups of people who opposed you that the aftermath of the election is an opportunity to forget what has happened in the past and to start things from scratch.

Maybe there are certain groups that have fought hard against you, and you will continue to disagree with them on major issues. While holding different views is part of politics, I suggest you nevertheless try to establish at least a channel of communication with them and that you think about what you can give them that does not cost you much politically. For example, I worked for a governor from the Green Party. He was elected, of course, to enact a pro-environmental agenda, and he did that. It was also clear that there would be interest groups that would disagree with his policies and try to fight them. That is the nature of politics. To deal with this, I advised him to establish a channel of communication with the leaders from those interest groups to reassure them that they would not be ignored. They would never turn into supporters of the governor, but he could at least soften the resistance. He got meaningful legislation done and was reelected convincingly.

In addition to good relationships, an incumbent needs outstanding staff. Some politicians yell at their employees, humiliate them, or throw things against the wall in their offices. As an external consultant, I am treated differently, but I have witnessed a fair share of such behavior myself, and it's a big mistake. The best preparation for your reelection is a high job approval rating, and no matter how well intentioned and skilled, no elected official can accomplish much alone. That said, I have also witnessed over the course of my career that the people around a leader have their own agendas with respect to policy, budget, or the attention of the principal. Having worked for several presidents, cabinet members, and other high-profile politicians, I have observed that senior staffers have several weapons at their disposal in order to move the politician in their desired direction. The first tool is overscheduling, sending the leader around to events that are not true priorities. That is, the places to visit are not chosen strategically and in the best interest of the principal, but in function of the staffer's own agenda. Since many politicians look for instant gratification, they don't object to a busy schedule, even if it is completely exhausting. These leaders soon act like lions hunting mice instead of going after antelopes. I have observed many times what happens as a result of this—they're constantly tired in meetings, then they lose their voice, and eventually, they get sick. There is a real connection between drowning in the very responsibilities and obligations of the office and losing focus on the big things. A second weapon is to withhold bad news, a point I talk more about in the next chapter. Finally, employees and allies can leak confidential information, mostly to try and influence policy decisions. Every US president in recent times has had to deal with this, and so have many high-profile politicians in other countries. Media articles with a quote like this will soon appear: "A high-ranking member of the administration, who spoke on the condition of anonymity, said that . . ." Leaks are particularly hurtful because they are anonymous and come from the inside. You might constantly wonder who the mole is among the people who sit with you at the table, look into your eyes, and tell you, "Yes, sir." Leaks might be the reason why some incumbents commit another big mistake, which is to surround themselves with yes-men. As a result, there is no challenge from the inside and no fresh blood within the team. This becomes more and more of a problem the longer the incumbency lasts. After some years in office, everyone in the administration and within the governing party owes their job to the incumbent, and therefore there is less and less internal criticism and challenge. If you think about it, politicians who commit big mistakes usually do so at the beginning or in the second half of their tenure. Power changes people, and sometimes this happens very rapidly. Many become cranky, thin-skinned, or plain arrogant.

One of the ways to prevent becoming out of touch is by making sure that those around you feel open to challenge you and push back on your ideas. This is sometimes the job that I'm brought in to do for an incumbent, because there are not enough people already doing so. When I start to work with incumbents, one of the first questions I ask is often how they think their reelection campaign will be different from the previous one. Observing their body language, I regularly notice that they never thought about it that way. To a certain degree, this is understandable. Few people think that they have to change right after having done something successfully. In that sense, it is always a temptation for successful politicians—which incumbents are by definition since they have won an election—to rerun the same campaign again. This is problematic for a number of reasons. First, you went from being a challenger who was free to criticize to being the one who has governing responsibilities and a record to defend. President Lula from Brazil compared this transition to getting married. He said that before the wedding, you promise your friends that everything will stay the same, but it is not true. Once married, you have responsibilities and you have to act accordingly.[147] It's the same in politics. Once you're in office, there are new constraints, you'll learn new information, and as a result, you will see many things differently. Second, it is also likely that in your reelection campaign, you will face a new opponent and, therefore, the way you will have to show contrast will be different. The electorate and the political demand have also evolved. Finally, it is also important to be aware of the fact that the media and technological context in which a campaign takes place changes rapidly nowadays. Within the time span of a few years, social media networks become deserted and new ones appear. A great campaign may therefore well include elements of a previous great campaign, but it should never be a simple rerun.

WHY DON'T YOU WIN REELECTION WITH 55 PERCENT?

Reelection campaigns are sometimes less glamorous and less emotional than challenger campaigns. Turnout is often lower, and they receive less press coverage. They are, however, no less fascinating or significant for the candidate. The more I have been involved in reelection campaigns myself, the more enthralling I personally find them. The reason for that is that as an incumbent you have unique possibilities to control things. The biggest asset of an incumbent is not the power of the office, no matter how high in the hierarchy. Your biggest strength is that you are distinctively well positioned to pursue a long-term plan, get media attention, and shape the political discourse and landscape. As a result, incumbent campaigns can and should be planned in a strategic and long-term manner. One of my longest standing clients, having consulted with him for more than fifteen years, is a mayor from a city with about one hundred thousand voters.

During that period, it happened several times that opponents literally moved out of the city after having lost repeatedly against my client.

Smart politicians start to plan their reelection campaign immediately after winning. In the old days, an incumbent would first govern for a while and only later start to worry about running for reelection and switch into campaign mode. This kind of thinking is obsolete given today's media environment and volatile public opinion. Nowadays, every day is election day, and you should try to win every day and especially every news cycle. I once advised a client who hired me to plan his reelection campaign even before he took the oath of office and started to serve his first term. Soon after winning, President George W. Bush set up a reelection team, consisting of the vice president and key advisers, who started to meet regularly right after moving into the White House. Setting up such a structure is crucial because whether we are talking about the White House, a state capitol, or the office of the mayor, all these organizations are designed to operate on a daily basis. There are plenty of employees, but it's no one's job there to plan long-term, let alone plan your reelection campaign. Most politicians do think about their own reelection constantly, but the risk is that decisions are made on a tactical level and on a day-to-day basis without a clear long-term strategy.

In recent years, many countries have become so polarized that even races with an incumbent running for reelection went down to the wire on election day. It doesn't have to be that way because as an incumbent you have a unique opportunity to break the tie if you take full advantage of the time in office. Or why don't you win reelection handily with 55 percent? This is not meant as a number that is chiseled in stone but as a concept. What I mean is that if incumbents do their work properly, they should sail to an easy reelection and win in a landslide. There are always factors that are outside of your control, but those put aside, the guiding principle should be the following: if you have a tough challenge during the reelection campaign, something went wrong during the time in office with respect to politics, policy, or communication, as my next example illustrates.

I once consulted with a congressman who hired me right after he won reelection. While he had prevailed on election day, he won less convincingly than he had expected. Having been in office for some time, he had enough political instinct to feel that something had gone wrong. I conducted baseline research for him consisting of a series of focus groups and a customized survey. The results clearly showed that he had not made the best use of his time and resources while in office. Voters felt that the incumbent failed to address a key issue. The events with the incumbent and his service to constituents also needed to be changed in order to have more impact. I made a series of recommendations regarding his communication, staff, and projects, and from there on, we started regular tracking. By the time the next election cycle arrived, his position had become much stronger. When the deadline for filing of candidacy had elapsed, no one had filed to run against him. One evening he called me up and said, "I am running unopposed. I guess that is not good news for you because I will not need your surveys during the campaign." I congratulated him on this political accomplishment but at the same time strongly disagreed that it was bad news for me. "What better reference could I wish for than to have you sail to reelection unopposed," I replied. It is true, and it should be the target of every incumbent to enter his reelection campaign in such a position of strength. To literally run unopposed may be difficult to accomplish in many cases, but even when there is an opponent, an incumbent should be in a position where the race is basically over before the actual campaign even starts.

German chancellor Angela Merkel was well known for her calm style of communication. When she ran for reelection in 2013, the economy was doing well and no one could imagine the refugee crisis that would soon hit Germany. Toward the end of the campaign, she faced off with her main opponent in a televised debate. The debate lasted for ninety minutes, and at the end of it, each one of the top two candidates had ninety seconds of uninterrupted time for their final statement. The takeaway from Merkel's statement was this: "you know me, we had four good years and now I wish you a nice evening."[148] Admittedly, that was not all she said, but this was the main point, and it was true. Voters knew her, the economy went reasonably well under her leadership, and voters were more or less satisfied with her performance. I like the statement because it perfectly illustrates how incumbents should run and close the deal before the actual campaign even starts. That reelection campaign was indeed over long before it started. On election day, Merkel's party, the CDU, won a landslide victory, taking 41.5 percent of the vote (a gain of 7.7 percent).[149] It was the high point of Merkel's career.

Another great illustration is the case of the British Labour Party and Tony Blair I wrote about earlier. I have also mentioned Philip Gould, one of the main architects of New Labour and its electoral wins. In an internal document, and while still in the opposition, Gould wrote that the modernization of the Labour Party should go beyond a single election campaign. "Labour has not just to win the next election: it must win a working majority," he wrote:

> It must have a project and policies that will transform Britain over an eight-year period; it must have a campaigning machine that will sustain Labour in power; it must become a party of sufficient structural and ideological coherence to support Labour in government, without splitting and without sabotaging.[150]

While in many other cases this would be mostly wishful thinking or abstract planning, it is actually pretty much what Tony Blair and the Labour Party did once they were in power. They governed as moderate New Labour and, most importantly, kept their promise of fiscal discipline. When it was time to run for reelection, the economy was performing well and unemployment was on the decline. Labour was seen as having kept and delivering on its key promises. Tony Blair himself summarized the message for the reelection campaign as follows: "a lot done, a lot to do, a lot to lose."[151] It was a short and simple message but full of content that reflected precisely what voters believed and wanted to hear at the time. "Do you really want to risk what Labour has accomplished?" It is always good to think about the framing of an election as a question you are asking the electorate, and this is a great example. On election day, the voters gave a clear answer. Labour lost only six seats and won again a huge majority of 413 seats in Parliament compared with 166 for the Conservatives and fifty-two for the Liberal Democrats.[152] At the time, it was the second-biggest win in the history of the UK, and Tony Blair would become the only Labour prime minister to serve two full consecutive terms.[153] If you look back at the campaign, it was never a real fight, but at the same time, the Labour Party also didn't do anything spectacular. It was reaping the benefits of the modernization effort it had carried out while in the opposition and stuck to its message and strategy. The media and observers therefore called it the "quiet landslide," a perfect example of how challengers turn into statesmen and sail to reelection.

THE NEED FOR A SIGNATURE ACCOMPLISHMENT AND HOW TO USE IT

Politicians usually get elected to do a specific thing. Call it a mandate. Once elected, you should immediately start to deliver on that key promise. If you are at least seen as trying to fulfill your key promises, your job approval ratings should remain relatively high. I always strongly suggest moving fast at the beginning on whatever it is that you want to do in office. Political capital is like raw fish. As soon as you get it, it starts to expire.

As a general rule, I also advise to get all the bad news out at the beginning. For example, if a cash check shows that there is less money in the bank than you thought, communicate that early while you can still hold your predecessor accountable for it. Put differently, whatever you want to blame on your predecessor, you have to do it quickly. With the passage of time, the bad circumstance you inherited will be your problem and blaming your predecessor will be seen as a lame excuse. Once the bad news is out, I suggest you spread the good news in small doses over the entire duration of your term. If you plan investments in education or an increase in pensions, spread these bits of good news out over a maximum amount of time.

It's also tremendously helpful for an incumbent to have what I call a flagship or signature accomplishment. This can be a key project, initiative, or legislative accomplishment. This naturally means that you need to get something meaningful done, and ideally, it is something that a majority of voters like. You also need to actively and repeatedly claim credit for it. For instance, when Barack Obama ran for reelection, a key part of the campaign's rationale for why he should be reelected was that he had saved the US automobile industry and had been instrumental in killing Osama bin Laden. For both, he did not do it personally, nor alone, but he played a central role and could claim credit for it. Business consultant Alan Weiss says that "credit never goes unclaimed."[154] He's right, and it applies to politics as well. If you do not grab it, someone else will. Once you have a flagship, you therefore need to constantly own, polish, and defend it. When I talk to clients, I tell them that they should celebrate their flagship, meaning that they need a communications plan to let voters know about it—particularly to let them know about the role they played in making it happen.

I once worked for a local executive, and one of his flagships was a hospital that was built during his time in office. This was something that voters had been asking for in our focus groups for some time and they were very much looking forward to finally getting it. The new hospital became the centerpiece of all communication, which started during the construction. Big signs leading trucks to the construction site had the side effect that voters also knew the hospital was being built. Important steps during the construction and especially the inauguration were major events. In this case, adding a new department to the hospital was an excellent way to polish the flagship and keep it in the news. That said, flagships have a life span. Even with the best communication plan, voters will ask for something new after a certain amount of time, but an imaginative PR effort can extend that life span considerably. I have worked for a senator who used his flagship as a central piece of his communication and campaigns for more than a decade.

The reason that you need a signature accomplishment is not that it would in itself always be enough to win a second term. If it's a big achievement, it could be. A more cautious hypothesis is, however, that voters rarely head to the polls in droves to say thank you. A signature accomplishment is important to make a new promise credible. If a politician has not fulfilled his last promise, how could voters believe he will deliver on the next one? I remember how I once talked to a client who was a city mayor. When he ran for his second reelection, things went pretty well in his city. His approval rating, his score in the reelection question, and his vote intention were all high, yet he was exhausted. "Voters always want more," he said. I'm afraid it's true.

After delivering on their mandate, incumbents should, therefore, quickly reinvent themselves and be seen addressing the new issue of the day. As new demands inevitably arise on the political horizon, an incumbent has to evolve with the electorate and stay alert. Old issues become settled, and new ones arise. When I became politically active during the 1990s, for example, illegal drugs were a huge issue in Switzerland. Today, this issue is more or less under control and has disappeared from the political agenda. As a politician, it is important not to fall out of sync with the mainstream. You do not want to come across like a suit from ten years ago that once was fashionable but now looks worn out. On the contrary, a reelection with 55 percent of the vote is achieved by delivering success while governing and defining future successes on your own terms, by always placing a new carrot ahead on the path for people to chase after. The advantage of this approach is that incumbents can influence what that carrot is and therefore control their own destiny vis-à-vis their reelection.

History is nonetheless full of leaders who failed to adapt to the changing political demand. What strikes me the most is that some of them actually performed well delivering on their initial mandate but were then voted out of office after that. After World War II, Winston Churchill was a hero and widely respected, yet he went on to lose reelection. Voters thought that Labour would be better suited to address the domestic issues facing the country. In the US, George H. W. Bush had skyrocketing approval ratings of more than 90 percent after the first war in Iraq, only to lose reelection to a young, unknown governor from Arkansas named Bill Clinton. Voters preferred him over Bush to fix the economy. In the UK, Boris Johnson ran to get Brexit done. It was a simple and clear promise. At the polls, Johnson won a landslide victory, with the Conservative Party getting the highest vote share and number of parliamentary seats in decades. After some time in office, Johnson's problem became that, well, he did get Brexit done. I call this the success trap for incumbents. After Brexit, there was no new big, defining idea. Instead, Johnson increasingly looked like a leader that enjoyed the perks of the office and was merely trying to hold on to it. His own party mates started to feel that Johnson was not the best bet to lead them into the future, and they forced him to step down. Go figure: in politics, people forget really fast.

THE KEY TO WINNING WITH 55 PERCENT: TRIANGULATION

A great modus operandi for incumbents to evolve, adapt to new trends, and absorb new issues is *triangulation*, a concept first used by US political consultant Dick Morris.[155] In short, it means to combine the best and most-liked policy proposals from the various political spectrums, and it is crucial to winning with 55 percent in a world that changes rapidly. Morris says convincingly that because of the party's ideologies, voters have to choose between entire programs. He compares it to restaurants that have only fixed menus and do not offer à la carte meals. Maybe a customer really likes the first course and the main course but would enjoy a different dessert. Another client wants the main course and dessert but a different first course. In other words, voters should not have to choose between the program of party A and the program of party B but get what they like best from each one. In US politics, for example, swing voters might like lower taxes, a classic Republican issue, and favor more investment in education, a typical Democratic advocacy. They might be in favor of more liberal abortion rights, a Democratic issue, but want to be tougher on immigration, a Republican stance. Outside of the US, a great example of triangulation is Tony Blair and the position he took on crime back when he was still the shadow home secretary. His tagline became that he wanted to be tough on crime and be tough on the causes of crime.[156] Traditionally, the right would call for more police and stricter punishment to crack down on crime, while the left would call for more investment in social work, schools, and after-school programs in order to prevent crime. Well, ideology and dogmatism aside, the two are not mutually exclusive, but voters can get both.

Another master of triangulation is Sebastian Kurz, former chancellor of Austria and former leader of the Austrian People's Party, *Österreichische Volkspartei* (ÖVP). As mentioned, Kurz rose to the top of his country's government at the age of thirty-one. He took a clear anti-immigration stance, and once elected, he formed a coalition with the populist Freedom Party of Austria, *Freiheitliche Partei Österreichs* (FPÖ). That coalition ended abruptly when a secretly recorded tape was published, in which the leader of the Freedom Party and Kurz's coalition partner was shown talking about possibly corrupt behavior. Early elections were called, and Kurz's ÖVP emerged with a big victory. Kurz saw himself in the comfortable position of having several options to form a new governing coalition. He chose the Green Party, which was known as part of the political left. A coalition between the ÖVP and the Green Party was a novelty in Austria and obviously quite a change from Kurz's first coalition. When the new government was announced, Kurz's message was that they wanted to protect the borders (his classic advocacy) and the environment (the main issue of the Green Party) at the same time.[157] In other words, this was not a coalition with the smallest common denominator, as is often the case in coalition governments, but was supposedly a combination of the best from both political worlds. It was classic triangulation, carried out by a masterful politician.

In essence, triangulation is the bridge connecting your mandate and flagship to future accomplishments. That is, it's a strategy of flexibility that allows you to shift from one goal to another one without losing the support of your base. Let's compare this approach of triangulation with cases such as former US president Donald Trump and former Brazilian president Jair Bolsonaro, who both lost their respective reelection campaigns. Both were extraordinarily effective in mobilizing and turning out their base and came closer to winning reelection than what polls indicated and most pundits predicted. If they had triangulated a little bit, they could well have prevailed.

HOW THE LAST US PRESIDENT TO WIN REELECTION IN A LANDSLIDE DID IT

A particularly enthralling case on how presidents win reelection in a landslide is Bill Clinton. When Clinton first ran for president in 1992, it was a classic challenger campaign as described throughout this book where change was defined as improving economic conditions. During his announcement speech, Clinton mentioned the "forgotten middle class" or "hardworking Americans" more than ten times, and one could argue that his entire campaign was an appeal to the middle class, their values, and their concerns. Clinton positioned himself as an outsider to the national leadership of his own party and used his humble personal background and his record as governor of Arkansas to portray mainstream values and make voters comfortable with the idea of a change in leadership. On election night, he won convincingly and ended twelve years of Republican reign.

That said, the success ended abruptly. Bob Woodward, an investigative journalist and author of more than a dozen bestsellers on US politics, describes the difficult first years of the Clinton administration. After moving into the White House, Clinton was seen as indecisive and voters could not identify him with a clear plan for the country, let alone a signature accomplishment. One of his main initiatives was health-care reform, which became highly unpopular and stalled in Congress.[158] Only two years later, when Americans headed to the polls for midterm elections in 1994, Clinton's Democratic Party suffered a heavy defeat. They lost fifty-two seats in the House of Representatives and eight seats in the Senate. This win was truly historic as it allowed Republicans to control both chambers of Congress for the first time in decades.[159] While President Clinton was not on the ballot himself, he was nevertheless associated with his party's loss. In addition to local issues and the congressional candidates, midterm elections are always also an opportunity for voters to express their opinions about the sitting president. Clinton's approval rating had dropped below 50 percent, which is commonly seen as an indication of an incumbent in trouble.[160] At the time, few observers thought that Clinton could recover and win reelection. The new Speaker of the House of Representatives at the time, Newt Gingrich, had successfully nationalized the House elections by presenting a platform called the Contract with America. In it, Republican candidates had put forward a series of proposals such as balancing the budget, tax cuts, welfare reform, Social Security reform, and term limits.[161] All proposals had previously been tested, and at least 60 percent of the voters approved of them. More controversial issues were left out. In the Contract with America, Republican incumbents and challengers also pledged that they would bring all proposals to a vote on the floor within the first hundred days should they become the majority. Once they were in command, the new Speaker and the Contract with America received tremendous media attention. It was the typical new kid on the block phenomenon. In addition to that, Republicans could launch painful investigations into the Clinton White House, leading to more bad press for Clinton and, as it would turn out, serious legal, political, and financial trouble.

As Republicans took the center stage in Washington, DC, President Clinton had to figure out a strategy for how to deal with it and stay politically relevant. The reflex of many in his shoes would have been to position themselves as the antithesis of the Republican majority in Congress. Clinton, however, took some time to come up with a plan. He hired consultant Dick Morris, who I mentioned earlier and who had worked with him years earlier when he was still the governor of Arkansas. Morris advised Clinton to, by and large, let Republicans do what they were elected to do.[162] According to Morris, Republicans traditionally had four issues on which they were strong: the deficit, crime, welfare, and taxes. If Clinton let Republicans do what they wanted, it would take these traditional Republican weapons off the table and thereby neutralize Republicans. Once the

Republican issues were dealt with, Clinton could then run—and win—on the issues on which he was strong, namely education and the environment.[163] Remember what we discussed earlier: to agree makes something a nonissue. The approach convinced Clinton, and it became his guiding strategy leading up to the election, including the guiding principle that he would only object to Republicans selectively.

A specific illustration of that approach was the fight over a balanced budget, a key component of the Contract with America. Clinton did not oppose it per se but tried to frame the debate as a discussion on how to balance the budget. Regarding the substance, Clinton's stance was not radically different from what Republicans wanted. He argued that by taking a bit more time to balance the budget, it was possible to accomplish it without cuts in social programs that were too drastic. As a result of that positioning strategy, he was able to portray Republicans as mean, slashing social programs and ignoring education and the environment.[164]

In hindsight, it almost seems to me as though the Contract with America gave Clinton a topic and forced him to clarify his communication on why he was president and what his plan and priorities were for the future. During the confrontation with Republicans, Clinton and his team also launched a major effort communicating his positioning and messaging. The goal was that Clinton would appear as rising above partisanship and look like a statesman bringing different sides together. A key component of that communication effort became a series of signature speeches, especially his State of the Union addresses. Clinton did not want to rely on speeches and earned media only; he also launched an early TV advertising campaign. The ads started to air more than a year before the election and did not call to vote for Clinton but instead communicated his positions and priorities.[165] It's a classic example of what I earlier described as winning every day. The effort was unique in the sense that I do not know of any other president who ran ads so early and so consistently.

The spots were aired in swing states. A particular focus was on states with moderate Republican senators, whereas media markets that were known to contain many journalists, such as New York or Los Angeles, were left out. The decision on which specific media markets to invest in was based on a sophisticated model including the following variables: previous voting history, advertising cost, estimated number of undecided or persuadable voters, likely impact on the Electoral College and congressional elections, and cumulative amount of previous Clinton ads.[166] President Bill Clinton personally edited and approved the scripts, which had an important side effect: the early advertising effort also led to more message discipline in the White House and for President Clinton himself. Going through the exercise of editing the ad copy helped Clinton crystallize his own message.[167]

By the time the campaign season was approaching, Clinton had delivered on most of what mainstream voters could reasonably expect from their president, and the race was basically over. Clinton defeated his Republican opponent Bob Dole by more than 8 percent in the popular vote. Clinton carried thirty-one states and beat Dole with 379 to 159 votes in the Electoral College.[168] It was the materialization of a landslide that was created before the actual campaign had started. After the midterm election, Clinton adapted to the political demand, neutralized Republicans, and communicated his priorities in a massive communication plan that was carried out over many months. If you want to increase your chances to be in a similarly strong position, you should start to plan your reelection strategy immediately after winning. You should try to win every day and every news cycle. You should deliver rapidly on your mandate and develop and polish your signature accomplishment. After that, you should adapt and use triangulation to address new demands without losing your base.

LAST PIECE OF ADVICE

Another thing that incumbents can and should do early on is to raise tons of cash. If new candidates hate to ask other people for money, who then in turn feel free to give advice and lecture the candidate, incumbents despise it even more. In most cases, an incumbent has better opportunities to raise money than a challenger, and it therefore makes sense to maximize it. As I mentioned earlier, a fundraising advantage is not a guarantee of success in itself, but it can be of tremendous help during the campaign. Through paid media, money buys presence, allows a campaign to be innovative and try out new things, and likewise gives strategic freedoms. An additional positive side effect of money is that it scares off potential rivals, including internal ones, from even running. In the US, all incumbent presidents who ran successfully for reelection in recent times have agreed to an extensive and early fundraising operation. Bill Clinton, George W. Bush, and Barack Obama, along with their spouses and their vice presidents, were all willing to commit their most precious resource to the effort—time. I wrote earlier in this chapter about how President Bill Clinton launched an early television advertising campaign. While the campaign was, without any doubt, effective and a key factor in his ultimate reelection win, it was also expensive. In other words, launching the TV advertising campaign had serious implications for Clinton's fundraising needs. He nevertheless agreed to it and was willing to do what was necessary, and a series of exclusive fundraising events were planned.

9

HOW VULNERABLE INCUMBENTS SURVIVE (BUT ONLY IF THEY DESERVE TO)

I have had clients whose careers were resurrected from the political grave. In this chapter, I share my insights on how vulnerable incumbents can launch an effective comeback and survive. It is certainly best for an incumbent to never be in such a position, and if you follow the strategies discussed in the last chapter, you should have strengthened your own position and not have a competitive reelection campaign. Unfortunately, some incumbents do not use their time in office effectively, encounter unfavorable (economic) circumstances, or face a challenger with tremendous appeal. Other incumbents have pushed for unpopular policies out of conviction and are paying a price for it in terms of popularity. Some incumbents simply lose touch with the electorate's mood and can't find the pulse of the people they supposedly serve. If an incumbent is truly vulnerable, it often is because of a combination of these factors. After all, power is something that can easily wear one out.

WHO TELLS THE EMPEROR HE IS WEARING NO CLOTHES?

The first step to a turnaround is a brutally honest assessment of where things stand. This is easier said than done because politicians—incumbents, in particular—are often surrounded by people who tell them what they think the politician wants to hear. The longer an incumbent is in office, the more this becomes an issue. I have worked for several presidents and I can confirm that conversations usually end with the same three words: "Yes, Mister President" or "Yes, Madam President." Let's face reality—it is awfully difficult to give powerful people bad news.

A vice president who was running for president sat together with his closest allies, some of whom were other local politicians. The vice president asked one of his supporters, a congressman, how he was doing in the congressman's home province. "It's close," the congressman replied, trying to soften the blow for his principal. In the province in question, the vice president was losing. It was not close.

This begs the question, whose responsibility is it to tell the emperor that he is not wearing any clothes?

It's certainly true that people are not always withholding bad news out of malice. It is human nature to want to please others. As mentioned in the previous chapter, people in power sometimes also become short-tempered or have real outbursts. As a result, the people around them are simply afraid to give bad news. As an external consultant, I am sometimes hired by in-house advisers to tell the principal the bad news. This is also why I think that it's my professional obligation to tell a client the truth. With prospective clients, I might nod politely even if I think that they are totally on the wrong track. Once I am hired, though, I'm brutally honest, and I think that this is actually one of my selling points. Some of my clients have multiple pollsters. The results from one are used to leak to the media, for fundraising, and to make themselves feel good, and then they know that they get the true results from me. In order to plan an effective comeback, reality is the best and only starting point. You can't plan and launch an effective comeback campaign in denial.

I once worked for a mayor of a city with more than one million voters. He was in deep trouble. Gearing up for reelection, the team probably felt that things were not going well, so they brought me in. When I presented results from a survey and a series of focus groups, only the closest allies were in the room: the mayor's spouse, a longtime friend, and a key adviser. At the start of the presentation, they all reached for their cigarettes, and by the time I had finished, there was so much smoke that you could hardly see across the room. Almost two-thirds of the electorate thought that the city was on the wrong track, and a majority of the voters disapproved of the job the incumbent mayor was doing. In the vote, the incumbent trailed the challenger by more than 20 percent. Among many other things, the incumbent had enacted several unpopular taxation policies, which I advised they stop immediately; voters were clueless about the incumbent's key achievements; and I recommended drastic measures with respect to health and policies of law and order. My presentation took place the day before Christmas, and the team later told me that this was their worst Christmas ever. The shakeup was nonetheless necessary to make an ultimate comeback possible. On election day, the incumbent surprised many by winning a second term.

THE KEYS TO A COMEBACK

A key part of the initial assessment I conduct in such a situation is to find out if voters are still willing to listen to the incumbent. It's absolutely crucial to have accurate public opinion research in order to do that: in particular, focus groups. Candidates matter, and outstanding politicians have personal or sometimes even emotional connections with the electorate. If times are bad for an incumbent, with a strained economy, low approval ratings, or scandals, it is key to still have that relationship. If voters remain willing to listen to the incumbent, this opens a window for a comeback. If, on the other hand, voters have made up their minds and are no longer listening to the incumbent, a comeback becomes difficult. Sometimes, the mood even turns into a personal, emotional dislike of the incumbent. If voters in focus groups describe a politician as a crocodile, alligator, or rat, that's a sign of great danger. If respondents are explicitly mean and, for example, describe a politician as fat, while that would not bother them in other situations, I take it as an indication of a personal aversion. In such a situation, the incumbent probably can't restore his approval rating while in power and is bound to lose reelection. I compare this to a romantic relationship: if one of the two clearly feels deep inside that the relationship is no longer the right thing, there is truly little the other one can do to prevent a breakup from ultimately happening. No number of gifts nor the most flowery words will change the other's mind in a sustainable way. If an incumbent is in such a situation, the divorce becomes unavoidable, and he can only repair his image sometime after leaving office. I have turned down serious business from politicians who have approached me too late. There is no point for me to start an operation when the patient is dead. If they lose, they will only blame it on me.

If there is a chance for a comeback, however, here are the keys to unlock it:

- *Acknowledge the pain*: We established earlier that incumbents represent the status quo. If an incumbent has a close race, then a substantial part of the electorate is, by definition, unhappy with how things are going. If the incumbent is simply ignoring that, or worse, tells voters that they are wrong, there is a serious risk of a disconnect. If voters are worried about crime, it's not the time to claim that statistics show no increase. Or, if the electorate is concerned about inflation, it's not wise to point to economic data that paint a rosier picture. Incumbents have to show that they (still) understand what voters experience. A key component of many comebacks is, therefore, to acknowledge the pain the electorate is feeling. As I said in the previous chapter, an incumbent campaign has to be different from a challenger campaign. This applies even more to a vulnerable incumbent.

- *Take responsibility*: While acknowledging pain is the minimum to reboot a relationship with voters, it may not be enough. Many situations will require self-criticism or even an apology for voters to consider giving the incumbent a second chance. Let me give you an example that I have observed several times. Politicians are under pressure, for example, on crime or immigration and then acknowledge the fears voters have. Voters might, however, not be afraid of immigration but disagree with the incumbent's policy on the matter. That's two different things. A politician that simply wants to listen to voters and then explain to them that what they are experiencing is wrong will come across as arrogant. A vulnerable incumbent definitely has to take more responsibility and be more responsive than that. Depending on the culture of a country, an apology can be explicitly said aloud, or it can be done implicitly by a course correction. During the COVID-19 pandemic, for example, I worked for a local executive who implemented a strict lockdown with steep fines. When he hired me to conduct focus groups, it turned out that voters were clearly unhappy. The policy was not explained well to them, and as a result, the incumbent was in danger of losing for the first time. He changed the policy and later on enacted many social services to help people get relief from the pandemic. The course correction, and the implicit apology it communicated, was not lost on voters, and my client won the election.

- *Fight back issue ownership*: A standard question we ask in surveys is which candidate or party voters trust more on a particular issue. In most election campaigns, there is one dominating issue, and ideally, the research shows that voters trust you more on that problem than the competition. In other words, you own that issue. In a setting with a vulnerable incumbent, the most important theme for voters is, however, often a driving force of the discontent and therefore a strength for the challenger. Put on the defense, incumbents often try to sit it out or downplay it. It's usually a mistake and more advisable to aggressively fight to win back issue ownership. The most promising tactic to accomplish that is often to shift the conversation from casting blame on the status quo to who has the best plan for the future.
- *Go on the offense*: I know that this may sound counterintuitive, but the most promising strategy for a vulnerable incumbent is often the relentless counteroffensive. The essence of the strategy goes like this: no matter how dissatisfied you are with how things are going, no matter how much you dislike the incumbent government, things will only get worse with the opposition. You argue that this is the wrong time for a change, that it has a high risk, or that a change would mean going back to old, failed policies. The key here is to try and reframe the election as a binary choice between two candidates rather than a referendum on the incumbent. George W. Bush and Barack Obama both won reelection pursuing that strategy.
- *Turn out the base*: an effective comeback includes closing the ranks and reenergizing the base. They might be disappointed that the incumbent could not fulfill all previous campaign promises, but

if there is still a personal connection with the top candidate, it is possible to remobilize the base.

AFTER TWELVE YEARS IN POWER, ASK FOR ANOTHER FOUR

One of the greatest comebacks in history is Helmut Kohl in Germany, who first became chancellor in 1982. By the time he was running for reelection in 1994, he had governed Germany for twelve straight years. Tremendously important things had happened during that time: the reunification of East and West Germany was a historic achievement, and at the same time, important steps were taken with respect to European integration with the creation of the European Union. Kohl deserved great credit for both. When he approached reelection, the mood of the electorate had nonetheless changed. Instead of feeling a patriotic high about the German reunification, voters were increasingly concerned about the cost of the undertaking and its slow pace. It was also the first time that Kohl had to defend his record during bad economic times, and after more than a decade, many voters simply wanted a new chancellor.

Kohl was nevertheless able to launch a comeback, and he did so almost single-handedly. It's a fascinating case, which I researched as part of my doctoral studies.[169] The catch-up started when his party, the CDU, met for its yearly convention. Kohl had never been considered a particularly good public speaker, but he used the exposure of the convention to deliver an electrifying speech.[170] It unified and mobilized his party. Kohl accomplished this with the right mix of self-criticism, taking credit for accomplishments, and drawing contrast with the opponent. When reading the speech, it struck me how aggressively, after more than a decade in power, Kohl claimed that his party was the party of the future.[171]

Later that year, and a few months before Kohl was up for reelection, the elections for the European Parliament took place. At the time, those elections were not considered particularly important, but Kohl was nevertheless heavily engaged in the campaign and toured the country. When the results from the European elections came in, Kohl's CDU was among the winners, while the opposition lost badly. To be on the winner's side further energized Kohl's camp and showed that winning reelection was also possible.

To answer the question of why he needed four more years and what his plans for the future were, I remember how Kohl said that he wanted to finish the reunification of Germany under the roof of a unified Europe, meaning the European Union. It was a masterful example of threading two generational projects into a single sentence, and Kohl argued (rather convincingly) that only he could finish these two projects. While the campaign material was highly patriotic and focused on Kohl as the chancellor of German reunification, it was also clear that simply reminding voters of the historic achievement of the reunification would not be enough to turn things around. For many voters, the economy had become the main worry in their daily lives. Instead of ignoring the economy as an issue, Kohl actively claimed it. He did not sugarcoat the state of things but left no doubt that he would be the best choice to improve it.

Toward the end of the campaign, Kohl and the CDU went on the offense. In Germany, people vote for parties, but these parties ultimately govern together in a coalition. During the campaign, possible coalition agreements are often being discussed. Kohl accused the rival SPD of possibly wanting to enter a coalition with the Party of Democratic Socialism, *Partei des Demokratischen Sozialismus* (PDS). The latter was the succession party of the Socialist Unity Party of Germany, *Sozialistische Einheitspartei Deutschlands* (SED), that had ruled East Germany during the Soviet era. While entering a coalition with the PDS was certainly not the plan of the SPD, it had not yet categorically ruled out any such cooperation. The genie was out of the bottle, and Kohl exploited it masterfully.[172]

Over the course of the campaign, a stunning turnaround took place in public opinion regarding Kohl as a leader and the state of the economy. A year before the election, two-thirds of the electorate had a negative outlook on Germany's economic situation while one-third had a positive one. By the time Germans were heading to the polls, this reversed and 66 percent of the voters had a positive economic outlook.[173] Kohl was also able to overtake his rival in the surveys with respect to which leader would be preferred as chancellor.[174] This is remarkable as I can't think of any other president or prime minister who, after twelve years in power, has fallen so low in public approval and yet was able to recover while still in office. It's also rare for an incumbent after so many years of public service to improve his campaign skills, but Kohl was able to do it. He started to use television to his advantage, and in particular the private channels that were new in Germany at the time.[175]

All the key elements of a comeback I mentioned above were part of Kohl's resurgent victory: acknowledging pain and taking responsibility, winning back issue ownership, going on the offense, and unifying and mobilizing the base. On election day, Kohl's CDU lost some votes compared with the previous election but was able to contain the damage. Thanks to an effective campaign, many voters that had voted for Kohl's party in the past but had started to take a look at the opposition came home to Kohl.[176] As a result, he was elected chancellor of Germany for the fifth time in a row.

WHEN DRASTIC AND DECISIVE MEASURES ARE NEEDED: WINNING REELECTION WITH RECORD HIGH UNEMPLOYMENT

If I were to ask you what tagline you associate with Barack Obama, you would probably answer with the tagline from his first presidential campaign, "change." This is not surprising because, as I wrote earlier, it was one of the best challenger campaigns ever. Once in the White House, Obama and his party pushed a controversial health-care reform through Congress. It was a big political accomplishment but also a key factor in why Obama soon turned into a polarizing figure himself. By that time, conservative media was thriving, such as the TV channel Fox News, for example. When Americans headed to the polls for the midterm elections, Democrats brutally lost sixty-three seats along with their majority in the House of Representatives.[177] Dan Balz, a journalist with the *Washington Post* and author of several books, describes the difficult context that Obama faced as he approached his reelection campaign. The budget negotiations with the new Republican majority led nowhere, and economic recovery from the financial crisis was far below expectations. According to the surveys, the economy was what voters were most concerned about, and the numbers did not look encouraging. No president in decades, before Obama, faced reelection with an unemployment level as high as 8.6 percent.[178]

Seizing control of the economic issue and turning out the base would be keys to Obama's reelection. Jim Messina, a political operative who previously served as the deputy chief of staff in the Obama White House, was tasked to manage Obama's reelection campaign. From the start, he and his team were fully aware of the fact that the economy would be a major vulnerability hanging around the president's neck like an anvil. Everyone worked under the assumption that this would be an awfully close election. Messina also insisted to his boss that the reelection campaign would be different from the previous one, and by all means, the team wanted to prevent the campaign from becoming a referendum on the economic performance of the Obama administration.[179] Passionate about public opinion research, the team launched a massive effort of listening to voters, which, in addition to numerous focus groups, also included a study where respondents were asked to journal their opinions of the economy. One of the main findings was that people were not dealing with a normal recession. What they were experiencing was rather a more fundamental and medium-term erosion of the middle class. Basic assumptions about the value of hard work, fairness, and opportunity seemed in doubt. For the campaign, these findings meant that the economy could be framed as a values issue. President Obama should not talk about the details of what he had done right or wrong with respect to economic policy, nor should he engage in a debate about the state of the economy and try to argue that it was better than what people felt in their daily lives. Instead, he should focus on his economic vision and values for the future. In other words, the campaign should be a debate about who would look out for the middle class. Instead of a referendum on Obama's performance on the economy, it should be a choice about economic values between Obama and his opponent. With respect to the president himself, the focus groups had revealed that while people were dissatisfied with the economy and felt that Obama had promised better, they had not closed their minds. In particular, opinions about his character were not compromised. Another important finding was that voters did not buy into the attack coming from Republicans that Obama had made a bad economy worse. This is an important point as it allowed Obama to fight back on the issue of the economy by reframing it as a values issue, showing contrast and going on the counteroffensive.[180]

Obama's opponent at the time was Mitt Romney, a former governor of Massachusetts who, in his early career, had made a fortune heading the private equity firm Bain Capital. The Obama team correctly assumed that Romney would make his economic competence the central rationale of his campaign. They therefore had to destroy that appeal, notably among middle- and lower-class voters. Months before the general election, the Obama campaign went on the attack. It began airing an ad called "Steel." The two-minute commercial told the story of workers from a steel plant that had been laid off after the company had been taken over by Bain Capital. In the ad, the former steel workers compared Romney to a vampire. Millions of dollars were sucked out of the plant before Bain Capital closed it, the workers claimed. Several details of the ad are noteworthy: it specifically stated that Mitt Romney was personally involved in the deal—something that I assume played well in focus groups. The ad also claimed that Bain sought the elimination of pension plans for the workers and the termination of their life insurance. "It was like watching an old friend bleed to death," one worker said in the ad. It ended with a highly emotional claim, stating that Mitt Romney was out of touch and didn't care about average people.[181]

The ad was not a lucky punch or a spontaneous idea. It was the result of a long process conducted by the Obama campaign. They had done extensive opposition research on Romney and had created a massive database. They looked in detail at everything Romney had said as governor of Massachusetts. They investigated his taxes and financial statements and his record as a businessman. During that process, the team found a way to turn his strength—economic competence—into a weakness. Yes, Mitt Romney may indeed have made millions as a businessman himself, but he did so by shipping jobs overseas at the expense of average workers.[182] In other words, according to the Obama campaign, Romney could not be part of the solution, because he was part of the problem.

The campaign reached the key decision to define Romney as early as possible before Romney had time and money to define himself. While that sounds obvious in hindsight, Mark Halperin and John Heilemann, two political analysts, explain that it was a delicate decision at the time. It meant that the campaign would spend money on advertising early on, which might have left the campaign short on funds later on. If the attack ads didn't work, the money would be gone, and Obama would risk being outspent during the closing of the campaign.[183] The gamble paid off, however. By summer of the election year, 52 percent of the voters had an unfavorable view of Romney, while only 37 percent had a favorable one.[184] As I mentioned in chapter 7, challengers are especially vulnerable to attacks.

Let's look at it from the viewpoint of the Romney campaign for a moment. The attacks hit him when he had just come out of a divisive primary and was cash-strapped. He could only start spending general election money once he was officially nominated as the Republican candidate at the Republican National Convention, which by then was still months away. He was faced with the decision to invest his remaining resources either in rebutting attacks, prosecuting the incumbent, or defining himself positively. I think that it was Romney's single biggest mistake as a candidate not to invest his own money in the campaign to defend himself against the ads. The team could also hardly have been surprised by the attacks as Romney's business dealings had been an issue in previous campaigns. While they may have been surprised about the vicious tone of the ad and the early timing, the allegation itself could hardly have had them stupefied. The Romney campaign produced a counter ad that told the story of another steel company that Romney had helped build, but it was only shown online.[185] I have had this painful discussion with several campaign teams myself—do not fool yourself. Responding to a TV ad with an online ad or a radio ad is the equivalent of not responding. You have to rebut an allegation at least as forcefully as the attack had been in the first place. It is also noteworthy that there was hardly any pushback by allied Republican groups, nor by Bain Capital itself. By the time Romney ran for president, he had become a distant memory to the team that was now running Bain Capital.[186]

A key factor for the success of the attack was also that President Obama himself personally went along with the strategy. I talked about this with David Plouffe, who had managed Obama's first presidential campaign and then served as a senior adviser in the White House. In an interview for this book, Plouffe explained that "incumbents cannot allow reelections to be a referendum on them. They have to make it a choice, but many don't like to do that."[187] He's absolutely right. Incumbents often think that if they just talk about their record and explain it better, they will win. This was not the case with Obama, who objected to some of the tactics but agreed with the game plan and therefore defended ads such as "Steel" in public. He argued that while investors want to make money, this would not make one qualified to talk about the economy as a whole.[188] "We don't need an outsourcing pioneer in the Oval Office," he summarized in a catchy way on the stump.[189] While no ad about Bain Capital tested better in focus groups than "Steel," it was by no means the only one that aired. A good attack campaign is rarely a single spot but a coherent narrative expressed through a series of ads. The Obama campaign also got help from Romney himself, who committed several gaffes with respect to unfortunate statements on the campaign trail or the handling of his tax returns. Without going into more detail regarding those, the learning here is this: if you have been hammering your opponent and it has an effect in the surveys, continue. If you enter the home stretch and a close race is still a tie, go on the offense and attack your opponent even harder.

Turning out the base was another crucial component of Obama's reelection campaign. "Obama's campaigns were grassroots first campaigns," David Plouffe told me. He emphasized that many politicians say that they want to build a grassroots campaign, but they don't invest in it.[190] Obama, with his background as a community organizer, was different and gave it the necessary time, attention, and resources. After winning in 2008, the campaign had an extensive debrief. It analyzed everything: number of field offices, door knocks, phone calls, volunteer-to-staff ratio, and more. Specific recommendations were made on how to further build on that already state-of-the-art operation.[191] This would soon become necessary. When team Obama started to plan the reelection campaign, their early polling showed that Obama still led his opponent in several key groups of the coalition that won him the White House the first time, such as women, Latinos, and younger voters. The challenge was a lack of enthusiasm. If these groups were to vote, they would overwhelmingly vote for Obama, but they needed motivation to turn out. An illustration for this lack of energy was the rally where the president launched his reelection campaign. The headlines stated that there were apparently empty seats in the stadium.[192]

That being so, Balz describes how the campaign launched probably the most ambitious technology and data analytics effort of any other campaign until that time. It also embraced and built on research from the political science community, which most other campaigns ignore. The goal was to analyze, model, measure, and track everything.[193] It was particularly interested in three specific target groups of voters:

- people who were not yet registered to vote but would likely vote Democratic
- people who had voted for Obama but did not vote in the midterm elections
- people who had voted for Obama but then voted Republican in the midterms[194]

Depending on the number of people in each category, every swing state had its own strategy. In some states, it would be enough to win if the campaign focused on registering likely Democratic voters and mobilizing previous Obama voters. In other states, these two groups would not be enough to win the state, and the campaign therefore also invested in convincing the third group.

The team also wanted to create a vast database that could integrate all information the campaign had about voters, donors, and volunteers. I am sure you have dealt with bureaucratic organizations, such as banks or hotels, where you have to fill out forms that provide information that the organization already had on you. The Obama campaign did the exact opposite. All information it collected would be put into one computer program and made available to those in the campaign who needed it. While Republican primary candidates were busy competing with each other, the Obama team used the time wisely, building the software that would run their database. In other words, a field worker in, say, Columbus, Ohio, should have access to all the data and information the campaign had about the voters in the area. This made volunteering easy. A volunteer could find out who among his Facebook friends and contacts would need to register to vote, who would need information on where to vote, and who would need some persuasion to vote for Obama. Such was the level of sophistication. Field workers and volunteers were also trained on how to use the data in addition to being taught how to interact with voters. In charge of field operations was, by the way, a certain Jennifer O'Malley Dillon, who would later run Joe Biden's successful campaign for president and become the second woman to lead a US presidential campaign to victory.[195] This being said, another point that strikes me as particularly important—despite the attention on models and data and its sophistication, the campaign managed to keep the focus on the fundamental strategic decisions. I have observed several times that there's a risk for campaign teams of getting lost in data to the point where it goes from being helpful to becoming a purpose of its own. That was not the case with the Obama campaign. As I have argued throughout this book, basic strategic decisions usually decide elections and not an accumulation of tactical moves. In that sense, the Obama campaign used technology and data to implement those decisions, one of which was a constant focus on reenergizing and turning out the base. On election day, Obama won reelection convincingly with 51.1 percent versus 47.2 percent for Romney. The result was even clearer in the Electoral College, which Obama carried with 332 votes, versus 206 votes for Romney.[196]

LAST RESORT: THE PRODUCTION OF HAPPENSTANCE

Another fascinating instance of a vulnerable incumbent surviving is when Gerhard Schröder ran for reelection as chancellor of Germany in 2002. The late social scientist Jens Tenscher correctly called it the production and presentation of happenstance.[197] When Schröder first ran for chancellor, his key message was the fight against unemployment. During the campaign, he had pledged that he would not deserve reelection if he were not able to significantly reduce the unemployment rate in Germany. By the time he approached the end of his first term in office, however, unemployment was still a major issue and Schröder was under pressure. While his government had launched several important reforms, there was also plenty of bad press. Schröder, his party, the SPD, and his government seemed already worn out. At the beginning of the election year, the main opposition party, the CDU, was clearly ahead of Schröder's SPD in the surveys.[198] During the course of the campaign, many doubted the election could still be turned around as there were few issues nor much good news to campaign on.

Two key topics turned out to be crucial for Schröder's comeback. At first, a flood of epic proportion hit eastern Germany a little over a month before election day. I mentioned in the chapter on crisis management that such an incident can be an opportunity for a political leader, and this was the case for Schröder. He was immediately present on the ground, showed empathy for the people who were affected, and was fast in promising and delivering help.[199] The flooding allowed him to portray himself as a man of action and to show contrast with his opponent. The opposition had nominated

Edmund Stoiber, the prime minister from the state of Bavaria, as their top candidate. When the flood hit, Stoiber was on vacation. To begin with, it is beyond me how a candidate for any election can go on vacation a couple of months before election day (and I have had this conversation with clients several times). To make things worse, Stoiber at first hesitated to interrupt his vacation because of the flood and accused Schröder of using it for campaigning purposes. He finally showed up on the ground several days later, only to face another problem: unlike the incumbent chancellor, he could not promise much concrete help.

In addition to the flood, the issue of the war in Iraq became crucial for Schröder's comeback. This was the time when US president George W. Bush planned a military operation to remove Saddam Hussein from power in Iraq and a so-called coalition of the willing could help the US accomplish that goal. Germany had supported a previous military campaign led by the US in Afghanistan, but another war, this time in Iraq, was unpopular with the public. As the matter started to be discussed in the media, Schröder again jumped at the opportunity and firmly declared that he opposed military action in Iraq.[200] What's important to point out in hindsight here is that the difference in substance between Schröder and the opposition was actually not all that big. It's not that the Christian Democrats advocated joining the military operation led by the US. While some people within the CDU did not exclude military action alongside its ally and under the mandate of the United Nations, many were also hesitant. The difference was in how categorically Schröder made his point. He sensed that the topic was working for him, and by repeating his crystal-clear opposition to any military action, he was able to frame the debate in his favor (and to divert attention from the unemployment issue). If voters wanted to be sure that Germany would not go to war in Iraq, they needed to vote for the incumbent government. On television, he declared:

> In such an existential question, there can only be a clear answer and no irresoluteness. I am against a military intervention, and I have mentioned the reasons for that [...] Once again, very clearly, no ifs and buts. I am against a military intervention in Iraq and under my leadership, Germany will not participate.*

Unwillingly, Stoiber attracted further media attention to the matter by continuing to talk about it. He basically said that he was also skeptical about the war but that Schröder was playing up fears and that his categoric refusal isolated Germany on the international scene.[201] Instead, he should have said that, of course, Germany will never go to war in Iraq, and now let us talk about the economy, the incumbent's record on it, and what to do differently.

Both issues—the floods and the controversy about the war in Iraq—also reminded voters what they liked about Chancellor Schröder. As a political person, he had always been more popular than his party and decidedly more liked than his rival. In a survey shortly before the election, 58 percent of voters preferred Schröder as chancellor compared with 34 percent for Stoiber. Voters also saw Schröder as more likable, more credible, more of a winner, and more able to lead the government than his opponent.[202] During the campaign, Schröder used this appeal to his advantage and actively framed the election as a choice between him and his rival.

The main event during the final weeks of the campaign was televised debates between the two candidates. While there had always

---

* "In solchen existentiellen Fragen gibt es nur eine klare Antwort und gibt es kein Rumdrücken. Ich bin gegen eine militärische Intervention und ich habe die Gründe dafür genannt [...] Noch einmal und ganz klar und ohne wenn und aber. Ich bin gegen eine militärische Intervention im Irak und unter meiner Führung würde Deutschland sich daran nicht beteiligen." "TV-Duell 2002: Schröder–Stoiber," Bundeszentrale für politische Bildung, accessed November 8, 2022, https://www.bpb.de/mediathek/video/339438/tv-duell-2002-schroeder-stoiber/.

been TV broadcasts with live discussions among politicians, a US-like duel between the two top candidates was about to happen for the first time in Germany. With an estimated fifteen million voters watching, the debates were by far the most viewed event of the campaign.[203] It turned out to be another key factor in Schröder's comeback. After the election, research showed that the debates helped mobilize less politically engaged voters to participate in the election, and more people saw Schröder as the winner.[204]

When all the ballots were counted, Schröder won a narrow victory. With 6,027 votes making the difference, it is fair to say that without an aggressive and well-run campaign, Schröder would likely have become a one-term chancellor.* Nowadays, public opinion has become so volatile and the media cycle so fast paced that one cannot simply roll out a campaign as we used to. While it's crucial to have a plan and a message in order to manage the chaos, we also have to stay alert to changing circumstances. In that sense, Schröder's campaign performance is remarkable and an example way ahead of its time. He wholeheartedly embraced opportunities that presented themselves to him. It's also noteworthy how late in the game the comeback took place. I remember how I followed the campaign myself at the time, and when I conducted research about it again for this book, one question haunted my mind: what would Schröder have done had the floods and the war in Iraq not have happened? After all, those events were barely on the radar screen beforehand. I have given this some thought, and I think the answer is this: as an

* The Green Party, Schröder's coalition partner, increased its vote share (+1.9 percent, 8.6 percent total). This is quite remarkable in the sense that it is usually difficult for the smaller coalition partner to shine. For Schröder, the fact that the Greens won votes was an important factor allowing him to continue the coalition between his Social Democrats and the Greens. Again, personality plays an important role here. The only politician who was more popular than Schröder was his vice chancellor from the Green Party, Joschka Fischer.

agile and astute campaigner, he would probably have found other opportunities on which to capitalize.

LAST PIECE OF ADVICE

Most comebacks include a ruthless counteroffensive. It's next to impossible to win a close election on the defense, let alone as a vulnerable incumbent. This has to be done extremely carefully, however. A vulnerable incumbent who attacks might not be seen as credible, and there is a high risk that already high unfavorable ratings further increase. In order to illustrate this, I want to go back to the case of Tony Blair and the British New Labour Party that was discussed in chapter 3. The Conservative Party reacted to the emergence of New Labour with a billboard that read "New Labour, New Danger."[205] It showed Tony Blair with red eyes like a demon. Philip Gould, one of the Labour strategists I introduced earlier, says that while the advertising admittedly got substantial media coverage, it was a strategic mistake. It conceded the fact that Labour had indeed changed and that there was a New Labour Party. In his focus groups, Gould found that there was nothing that voters feared about New Labour. If anything, voters were doubtful that New Labour was real and thought that it was only packaging and that once in power, Labour would go back to its old policies. In other words, the New Labour, New Danger campaign was based on a complete misreading of public opinion. Gould speculates that it would probably have been more effective for the Tories to cast doubt on the claim of New Labour and try to portray it as a sham. He says that the Tories could have beaten them by, first, directly and humbly apologizing for the tax increases that they had implemented. Then, they should have highlighted their own achievements, most importantly by owning the economic recovery that was taking place and by linking it to their actions and pointing out how it benefited average voters. The last point is important because Gould found in his focus groups that voters indeed saw the economy as improving but did not feel it in their own lives. Gould says, convincingly, that a "Don't Let Labour Blow It" campaign could have helped reduce Labour's margin more effectively than the one that the Conservatives had run. The Tories did attack Labour relentlessly but in a way that did not connect with voters. As a result, it backfired, and the Tories looked increasingly desperate and as though they were running out of ideas.[206]

10

FINAL WORD AND CHECKLIST

All my clients want the same thing—to win the election. If you have read this book, chances are that you are planning your first campaign for office or one that is crucially important for your career. Either way, it's a campaign that you will never forget throughout your life.

In some countries, presidents go straight from the presidential palace to jail and back to the presidential palace. Your journey might be less of a roller-coaster ride, but if you run for office, the highs can be really high. Candidates want to win, they want to win in a landslide, and they always want to appear as winning. They want to run unopposed or put the race behind them before the campaign even starts. They want to win while spending as little as possible. They want to be seen as close to the president, be a nationwide (or international) player, and be frequently interviewed by the media.

On the other hand, the lows as a candidate are really low. I remember how the spouse of a candidate who lost once told me, "You know, after our loss, I realized that in the end, it's my husband and me." All the other people suddenly stopped calling. Candidates are afraid of losing, or worse, of losing to their worst enemy. They are uneasy about well-funded or celebrity opponents. They worry about being cheated from victory or being betrayed and left standing in the rain by their own people. I remember how a candidate, after a long presentation of mine, told his wife to go away so that he could ask me his most sensitive question—whether his lead was big enough so that his win could not be stolen from him. Candidates are also afraid of becoming the target of attacks or the center of scandals in the media. I had coaching sessions where candidates confessed to me the headlines they fear the most. Candidates who trailed far behind have asked me if there is still a chance for them to win. No matter the lows, though, there is always hope. I've personally suggested to certain campaign teams to consider a graceful exit from a race, and yet they won on election day.

I once worked for a client who wanted to run for congress against an incumbent. We took a survey eight months before the election. The result was that more than half of the voters were either not aware of my client or had an unfavorable opinion of him. To make things worse, the incumbent was rather well-liked. He didn't have much hard support and voters were not overly impressed with his record, but he was in reasonably good shape. With respect to the vote question, the survey at the time had us trailing the incumbent 9 percent to 81 percent. After the presentation of the results and recommendations, I asked the client directly how sure he was that he wanted to push through with his candidacy. "One hundred percent," he said without hesitation, and off he went. He mobilized all resources and campaigned relentlessly. Less than a month before the election, I conducted a tracking survey for him. He had dramatically increased both his favorability and his vote share. He was now trailing the incumbent 36 percent to 44 percent. It was a big improvement but still looked like a long shot. Being the underdog playing offense, however, also has its advantages. The fighting spirit that says you have nothing to lose can be a great motivating force and unleash tremendous energy. On election day, my client won 52 percent to 47 percent. If he can do it, you can do it.

In this book, I have presented a model on how opposition candidates run effectively. They aggressively claim and own change, which is defined as improving the economy and passing major reforms. They are willing and able to put the incumbent on the defensive and counterbalance their call for change with an effort to reassure voters. They are able to unify their own party and political family and often engage in new alliances. They start to plan early, launch intense grassroots-like campaigns, and invest the necessary time in improving their campaign skills. I have mentioned Barack Obama's first run for the presidency as one of history's best challenger campaigns. His advertising campaign was led by Jim Margolis, who coherently and convincingly sums up their strategy as follows:

> The first imperative was that we needed to own change. Second, we had to focus relentlessly on the economy which we did throughout. Third, there was a dimension that was about reassurance. We needed to send the right cultural cues indicating that we were totally right on a lot of those values issues.[207]

If you think about it, that also summarizes my model. The essence of Margolis's words is found in every chapter of this book. If you apply them to your own circumstances, you will undoubtedly find yourself building a similarly strong campaign. Here's a checklist with twelve points by which you can assess yourself:

1. Is the incumbent really vulnerable? Elections with an incumbent are foremost a referendum on the incumbent. An honest assessment here will include the duration of the

incumbency, wear and tear of the incumbent, potential scandals, and the general satisfaction of voters with the status quo. I suggest you also compare the state of the incumbent with how he was during the last election and how comparable incumbents in other states or countries perform.

2. Assess your own challenger quality on the following dimensions:
   - your current awareness, favorability, and vote share
   - your previous campaign experience (have you had a tough election campaign?)
   - your political experience, knowledge, and command of the issues
   - your ability and willingness to self-fund or raise money that puts you at eye level with the incumbent
3. Do you know how many votes you need to win? You need to determine and write down a specific number. A local representative recently asked me what he should do with that number once he knew how many votes victory would require. The answer is to become obsessed with it. You should have a crystal-clear strategy on who these people are and all campaign activities should be geared toward that target audience. In other words, you can assess everything you plan, say, and do in your campaign through the lens of whether it helps you reach the votes you need to win the election.
4. What is your campaign message? I suggest you write down a paragraph in full sentences as in the examples I showed—not more, not less. Then you should ask yourself if this is what your target audience cares about and will likely care about until election day and if you are seen as a credible messenger for it.

5. In most campaigns, there is one deciding issue. Whatever that issue is in your case, ask yourself if voters really think you would do a better job addressing it than the incumbent. In other words, do you own that issue?
6. Do you fully maximize the advantages of a challenger (criticize the incumbent, be the new kid in town, build a movement)? Are you willing and able to show contrast with the incumbent that is favorable to you, both with respect to visuals and substance?
7. Make a list of your biggest weaknesses as a candidate. Then come up with an inoculation strategy, meaning a series of specific measures to neutralize them.
8. What is your plan to make voters comfortable to embrace change? I have discussed more than a dozen strategies such as key appointments, local or previous government record, patriotic and bipartisan rhetoric, policy moderation, and ideological distance from your own party. Your plan should involve at least half of them.
9. Do you have a plan for an aggressive outreach effort to unify your party, your political camp, and beyond that, to engage in a broad alliance? Are you willing to execute the plan and reach out, including to your intraparty competitors and critics?
10. Are you willing and able to launch a state-of-the-art, long, and intense campaign? Typical activities of candidates include giving speeches, giving media interviews, asking for money, meeting voters, and debating opponents. Are you honest about those that you are uncomfortable with, and will you invest the time to get better at them?
11. Does your advertising material effectively communicate your campaign message? Or is it empty of content and mostly pleasing you and your close supporters?

12. Who is running your campaign? The answer to that question should be one name, which is not you. The person should have some discretionary power over funds and staff. If your answer here is something different, there is a high risk your campaign will be a mess.

If you can honestly and objectively check off nine or more of these points, then you are in formidable shape. If you have four to eight issues under control, you have a lot of work ahead of you. If you are confident in less than four points, ask yourself if this is the right time for you to run. There is a considerable chance that you are dreaming. If your strongest and main point is the first one—the weakness of the incumbent—I must unpleasantly warn you: blunders and scandals alone are often not enough to beat an incumbent.

In addition to my clients, whose names I have kept to myself, I wrote about politicians such as Bill Clinton, Luiz Inácio Lula da Silva, Barack Obama, Emmanuel Macron, Donald Trump, Gerhard Schröder, Volodymyr Zelensky, David Cameron, and Tony Blair. It strikes me how differently their journeys have played out. At the time of writing, some are still in power and have reached new heights in popularity. Others are back in power after a successful comeback. Some have retired from politics and enjoy life as senior statesmen. Yet others have become very polarizing. They are nevertheless the best challengers and opposition candidates to study, and the odds are, if you're planning a challenging campaign, that the lessons of those leaders will provide precious insight.

There are times when I may have sounded Machiavellian throughout this book. I even poked fun at the newbies in politics who email me about how they want to save their district or state. In this final word of the book, I want to correct that impression a bit. Running for office can be and should be a noble enterprise. Admittedly, I'm more skeptical today about the ability to do good, big things in elected office compared with when I began my career as an activist more than thirty years ago. I do, nonetheless, certainly still subscribe to the notion that keeping the wrong people from getting elected can prevent bad things from happening. I'm also strongly convinced that avoiding bad policy decisions on key matters can prevent significant damage from occurring.

I will now leave you with a final piece of encouraging advice. There is a reasonable likelihood that voters who are undecided in the surveys shortly before election day break for the challenger. After I'm done with a campaign, I usually compare my last survey with the actual result, and it often shows this pattern. I once worked for a challenger who was running for congress against an incumbent. The challenger came from a known political family with longtime roots in the district, but the incumbent was also strong. We had timed the fieldwork for the last survey so as to have the results a few days before election day. The result was that my client led by 2 percent, which was within the margin of error. What really stood out to me was that a stunning 21 percent of respondents said that they were undecided. I presented the results late in the evening at the house of the principal. "I don't think these people are truly undecided," I said. After months of campaigning between two high-profile candidates, how could so many people have not made up their minds. "I think that most of them don't want to say whom they are voting for," I explained. A few days later, on election day, my client won an undisputed victory.

Think about it from the voter's point of view: if they have seen the incumbent in action for four years and are still undecided before election day, and if the incumbent is not running a counteroffensive campaign as I described in the last chapter, what new information could make them vote for the incumbent? If you have defined change as discussed, owned the deciding issue, and made voters comfortable with change, there is a good chance that you will win over many of those who are undecided. There have certainly been exceptions to this rule, but it has often played out like that. With a little hope and sweat and enough humility to make good decisions, you may find yourself the next great maker of change.

Now, off to the races.

ACKNOWLEDGMENTS

Many people have helped me write this book. First, I would like to thank my loyal clients. While writing, I realized how much we have accomplished together during the past seventeen years.

My friends Daniel Wiedmer, Brian Paler, Fabio Müller, and Thomas Würsch gave me precious input. Leonie Hürlimann helped me conduct initial research for the book. I thank Mark Fretz and Evan Phail at Radius Book Group for their support and patience. Sam Corden, Marji Ross, Helen Overmyer, and Eliza Dee have tremendously improved the manuscript during the editing stage. Thank you for your work.

Foremost, I would like to thank my wife and the love of my life, Katsiaryna. I have been talking about this book for more than ten years. It's no coincidence that I got it over the finish line now that you have entered my life.

NOTES

1. Joseph Napolitan, *The Election Game and How to Win It* (Brattleboro, VT: Echo Point Books & Media, 1972, 2017), 2–3.
2. "Jack Nicklaus Quotes: Learn the Fundamentals of the Game and . . . ," Inspirational Stories: The Power of Words, accessed August 25, 2022, https://www.inspirationalstories.com/quotes/jack-nicklaus-learn-the-fundamentals-of-the-game-and/.
3. "Reelection Rates Over the Years," Open Secrets: Following the Money in Politics, accessed February 5, 2023, https://www.opensecrets.org/elections-overview/reelection-rates.
4. "Public Attitudes Toward the War in Iraq: 2003–2008," Pew Research Center, March 19, 2008, https://www.pewresearch.org/2008/03/19/public-attitudes-toward-the-war-in-iraq-20032008/.
5. "Le coiffeur de François Hollande payé 9 895 euros brut par mois depuis 2012," *Le Monde*, July 12, 2016, https://www.lemonde.fr/politique/article/2016/07/12/le-coiffeur-de-francois-hollande-paye-9-895-euros-brut-par-mois-depuis-2012_4968564_823448.html.
6. Edward Mason and Tom Mashberg, "Mitt Has Always Plummeted in the Polls," *Salon*, December 9, 2011, https://www.salon.com/2011/12/09/mitt_has_always_plummeted_in_the_polls/.
7. Philip Gould, *The Unfinished Revolution: How New Labour Changed British Politics Forever* (London: Abacus, 2011), xxv.
8. Alastair Campbell, *Winners and How They Succeed* (London: Hutchinson, 2015), 13.
9. Theda Skocpol, *States and Social Revolutions* (Cambridge: Cambridge University Press, 1979, 2015).
10. Allan J. Lichtman, *Predicting the Next President: The Keys to the White House* (Lanham, MD: Rowman & Littlefield, 2020).
11. Lichtman, *Predicting the Next President*, 3.
12. James Carville and Paul Begala, *Buck Up, Suck Up…and Come Back When You Foul Up* (New York: Simon & Schuster, 2002), 86.
13. Ronald A. Faucheux, *Running for Office: The Strategies, Techniques and Messages Modern Political Candidates Need to Win Elections* (New York: M. Evans & Company, 2002), 141, 142.
14. "Exit Polls," *CNN*, accessed August 26, 2022, https://edition.cnn.com/election/2020/exit-polls/president/national-results.

15 "In Their Own Words: Transcript of Speech by Clinton Accepting Democratic Nomination," *New York Times*, July 17, 1992, https://www.nytimes.com/1992/07/17/news/their-own-words-transcript-speech-clinton-accepting-democratic-nomination.html.

16 Claude Estier, *Journal d'une victoire: François Hollande* (Paris: Cherche-midi, 2011), 143.

17 Author interview with David Plouffe, February 24, 2023.

18 "Transcript: Barack Obama's Acceptance Speech," *NPR*, Speeches from the Democratic National Convention, August 28, 2008, https://www.npr.org/templates/story/story.php?storyId=94087570.

19 "Transcript: Barack Obama's Acceptance Speech."

20 Author interview with David Plouffe, February 24, 2023.

21 David Plouffe, *The Audacity to Win: The Inside Story and Lessons of Barack Obama's Historic Victory* (New York: Viking, 2009), 103.

22 Kathleen Hall Jamieson, *Electing the President 2008: The Insider's View* (Philadelphia: University of Pennsylvania Press, 2009), 92–102.

23 "90 Percent," campaign TV ad, accessed August 26, 2022, https://www.youtube.com/watch?v=PluoMotgl2w.

24 John Heilemann and Mark Halperin, *Game Change: Obama and the Clintons, McCain and Palin, and the Race of a Lifetime* (New York: Harper Perennial, 2010), 375.

25 "Transcript: Barack Obama's Acceptance Speech."

26 "Still," campaign TV ad, accessed August 26, 20022, https://www.youtube.com/watch?v=bQ2I0t_Twk0.

27 "Transcript: Barack Obama's Acceptance Speech."

28 Michael Cooper and Michael Powell, "McCain Camp Says Obama Plays 'Race Card'," *New York Times*, August 1, 2008, https://www.nytimes.com/2008/08/01/world/americas/01iht-01campaign.14931438.html.

29 Jamieson, *Electing the President*, 98.

30 Plouffe, *Audacity to Win*, 323.

31 Heilemann and Halperin, *Game Change*, 377.

32 "Plan for Change," campaign TV ad, accessed August 26, 2022, https://www.youtube.com/watch?v=ONM7148cTyc.

33 Nick Lioudis, "The Collapse of Lehman Brothers: A Case Study," Investopedia, accessed August 26, 2022, https://www.investopedia.com/articles/economics/09/lehman-brothers-collapse.asp.

34 Steve Benen, "McCain Still Sees the Fundamentals of the Economy As Strong," *Washington Monthly*, September 15, 2008, https://washingtonmonthly.com/2008/09/15/mccain-still-sees-the-fundamentals-of-the-economy-as-strong/.

35 Sasha Issenberg, "McCain's Radical Candor," *Politico*, accessed August 26, 2022, https://www.politico.com/magazine/story/2018/08/26/john-mccains-radical-candor-219601/.

36 Jonathan Martin and Mike Allen, "McCain Unsure How Many Houses He Owns," *Politico*, accessed August 26, 2022, https://www.politico.com/story/2008/08/mccain-unsure-how-many-houses-he-owns-012685.

37 Ben Smith, "Obama: By McCain's Standard, $3 million Is Middle Class," *Politico*, August 18, 2008, https://www.politico.com/blogs/ben-smith/2008/08/obama-by-mccains-standard-3-million-is-middle-class-011049.

38 Thomas Evan, *A Long Time Coming: The Inspiring, Combative 2008 Campaign and the Historic Election of Barack Obama* (New York: PublicAffairs, 2009), 130, 131.

39 Author interview with David Plouffe, February 24, 2023.

40 "2008 Presidential Popular Vote Summary For All Candidates Listed on at Least One State Ballot," Federal Election Commission, accessed April 30, 2023, https://www.fec.gov/resources/cms-content/documents/tables2008.pdf.

41 "In Their Own Words: Transcript of Speech by Clinton."

42 "Full Text: David Cameron's Speech to the Conservative Conference 2005," *Guardian*, October 4, 2005, https://www.theguardian.com/politics/2005/oct/04/conservatives2005.conservatives3.

43 "Full Text: David Cameron's Speech."

44 Estier, *Journal d'une victoire*, 110.

45 "Announcement Speech," 4President.org, Presidential Campaigns and Candidates, October 3, 1991, http://www.4president.org/speeches/1992/billclinton1992announcement.htm.

46 "'92 Democratic Convention: Clinton Text: 'I Still Believe in a Place Called Hope'," *Los Angeles Times*, July 17, 1992, https://www.latimes.com/archives/la-xpm-1992-07-17-mn-3671-story.html.

47 "'92 Democratic Convention."

48 Gould, *Unfinished Revolution.*

49 Tony Blair, *A Journey* (London: Arrow Books, 2011), 89.

50 Blair, *Journey*, 30–63.

51 Blair, *Journey*, 197.

52 Blair, *Journey*, 49.

53 "Leader's Speech, Blackpool 1994," British Political Speech, accessed October 13, 2022, http://www.britishpoliticalspeech.org/speech-archive.htm?speech=200.

54 "Leader's Speech, Blackpool 1994."

55 Gould, *Unfinished Revolution*, xii.

56 Gould, *Unfinished Revolution*, xvii.

57 Aisha Gani, "Clause IV: A Brief History," *Guardian*, August 9, 2015, https://www.theguardian.com/politics/2015/aug/09/clause-iv-of-labour-party-constitution-what-is-all-the-fuss-about-reinstating-it.

58 Blair, *Journey*, 76.

59 Gould, *Unfinished Revolution*, 224.

60 Gould, *Unfinished Revolution*, 224.

61 Gould, *Unfinished Revolution*, 265.

62 Charlotte Tobitt, "Andrew Neil: Line Between Murdoch Press and State Became Blurred During Blair Era," *Press Gazette*, July 16, 2020, https://pressgazette.co.uk/rupert-murdoch-documentary-rise-of-dynasty-bbc-tony-blair/.

63 "1997: Labour Landslide Ends Tory Rule," *BBC News*, accessed April 28, 2023, http://news.bbc.co.uk/2/hi/uk_news/politics/vote_2005/basics/4393323.stm; "The Election. The Statistics. How the UK voted on May 1st," *BBC*, accessed

April 28, 2023, https://www.bbc.co.uk/news/special/politics97/news/05/0505/stats.shtml#detail.

64 Gould, Unfinished Revolution, 387.

65 "UK General Election 1997—Tony Blair's Victory Speech," YouTube, accessed October 8, 2022, https://www.youtube.com/watch?v=8bldWwrgS_E.

66 Louis Perron, *How to Overcome the Power of Incumbency in Election Campaigns* (Baden-Baden, Germany: Nomos Verlagsgesellschaft, 2010), 263, 264.

67 Sue Branford and Bernardo Kucinski, *Lula and the Workers Party in Brazil* (New York: The New Press, 2005), 25.

68 Richard Bourne, *Lula of Brazil: The Story So Far* (Berkeley: University of California Press, 2008), 56.

69 Bourne, *Lula of Brazil*, 72.

70 Wendy Hunter, *The Transformation of the Workers' Party in Brazil, 1989–2009* (Cambridge, UK: Cambridge University Press, 2010), 113, 114.

71 "Brazil. Presidential Election 1989," Electoral Geography 2.0, accessed March 17, 2023, www.electoralgeography.com/new/en/countries/b/brazil/brazil-presidential-election-1989.html.

72 Hunter, *Transformation*, 114.

73 Hunter, *Transformation*, 116.

74 Branford and Kucinski, *Lula and the Workers Party*, 81–85.

75 Author interview with Duda Mendoça, December 20, 2005.

76 Hunter, *Transformation*, 138.

77 Author interview with Duda Mendoça, December 20, 2005.

78 Hunter, *Transformation*, 137, 138.

79 Ted G. Goertzel, *Brazil's Lula: The Most Popular Politician on Earth* (Boca Raton, FL: Brown Walker Press, 2011), 35.

80 Hunter, *Transformation*, 140.

81 Goertzel, *Brazil's Lula*, 17.

82 Hunter, *Transformation*, 128.

83 Perron, *How to Beat the Power of Incumbency in Election Campaigns*, 176–80.

84 Hunter, *Transformation*, 79–105.

85 Branford and Kucinski, *Lula and the Workers Party*, 58.

86 Steven Derix with Shelkunova, *Zelensky: Ukraine's President and His Country*, trans. Brent Annable (Surrey, UK: Canbury Press, 2022), 93–98.

87 Adrian Karatnycky, "The World Just Witnessed the First Entirely Virtual Presidential Campaign," *Politico*, April 24, 2019, https://www.politico.com/magazine/story/2019/04/24/ukraine-president-virtual-campaign-226711/.

88 Serhii Rudenko, *Zelensky: A Biography* (Cambridge, UK: Polity Press, 2022), 6–8.

89 Rudenko, *Zelensky: A Biography*, 4, 5.

90 Derix with Shelkunova, *Zelensky*, 109.

91 Derix with Shelkunova, *Zelensky*, 115–119.

92 Derix with Shelkunova, *Zelensky*, 117.

93 Rudenko, *Zelensky : A Biography*, 12.

94 "Résultats de l'élection présidentielle 2017," Department for Internal Affairs, May 7, 2017, https://www.interieur.gouv.fr/Elections/Les-resultats/Presidentielles/elecresult__presidentielle-2017/(path)/presidentielle-2017/FE.html.

95 Pauline Théveniaud, "Présidentielle: comment Emmanuel Macron a créé sa machine à gagner," *Le Parisien*, April 23, 2017, https://www.leparisien.fr/elections/presidentielle/presidentielle-comment-emmanuel-macron-a-cree-sa-machine-a-gagner-23-04-2017-6880890.php.

96 François-Xavier Bourmaud, *Emmanuel Macron: Les coulisses d'une victoire* (Paris: Éditions de l'Archipel, 2017), 128.

97 "Je suis candidat à la Présidence de la République | Emmanuel Macron," YouTube, accessed November 14, 2022, https://www.youtube.com/watch?v=m528uyLhWnA.

98 Arnaud Benedetti, *Le coup de com' permanent* (Paris: Les Éditions du Cerf, 2018), 59–65.

99 "Flüchtlingspolitik: «Wir schaffen das»-Statement von Angela Merkel am 31.08.2015," YouTube, accessed May 6, 2023.

100 Markus Feldenkirchen, "Die Martin-Schulz-Story," *Spiegel Politik*, September 29, 2017, https://www.spiegel.de/politik/martin-schulz-die-story-seiner-gescheiterten-kampagne-a-00000000-0002-0001-0000-000153535177.

101 "Bundestagswahl 2017," Die Bundeswahlleiterin, accessed April 27, 2023 https://bundeswahlleiter.de/bundestagswahlen/2017/ergebnisse.html.

102 Perron, *How to Beat the Power of Incumbency in Election Campaigns*, 132–35.

103 Faucheux, *Running for Office*, 51, 52.

104 Kevin Breuninger, "Billionaire and Former Presidential Candidate Ross Perot Dies at 89," *CNBC*, July 9, 2019, www.cnbc.com/2019/07/09/billionaire-and-former-presidential-candidate-ross-perot-is-dead-at-89.html.

105 "Full Text: President Obama's DNC speech," *Politico*, July 27, 2016, https://www.politico.com/story/2016/07/dnc-2016-obama-prepared-remarks-226345.

106 "Exit Polls," *MSNBC*, accessed March 19, 2022, https://www.nbcnews.com/politics/2016-election/president/.

107 "Niedersachsen Landtagswahl 1998," *Tagesschau online*, accessed May 8, 2023, https://www.tagesschau.de/wahl/archiv/1998-03-01-LT-DE-NI/index.shtml.

108 "Adrian Amstutz gewinnt um Haaresbreite," *Tages-Anzeiger* online, March 6, 2011, https://www.tagesanzeiger.ch/adrian-amstutz-gewinnt-um-haaresbreite-468141034378.

109 Tara Golshan, "Bill Clinton's First Major Appearance at a Convention Almost Destroyed His Career," *Vox*, July 26, 2016, https://www.vox.com/2016/7/26/12285312/bill-clinton-dnc-1988-speaker-late-night.

110 Bill Clinton "In Closing," *C-Span*, July 20, 1988, https://www.c-span.org/video/?c4609785/bill-clinton-in-closing.

111 "How Bill Clinton Turned a Dreadful Convention Speech into Political Stardom," *Washington Post*, August 18, 2020, www.washingtonpost.com/outlook/2020/08/18/how-bill-clinton-turned-dreadful-convention-speech-into-political-stardom.

112 "You Can't Hire Someone Else to Do Your Push-Ups for You," Quotefancy, accessed on April 26, 2023, https://quotefancy.com/quote/837960/Jim-Rohn-You-can-t-hire-someone-else-to-do-your-push-ups-for-you.

113 "Jose Maria Aznar: 1953–: Prime Minister of Spain," Biography Jrank, accessed on April 26, 2023, https://biography.jrank.org/pages/3021/Aznar-Jose-Maria-1953-Prime-Minister-Spain-Assumed-National-Political-Role.html.

114 Joshua Green, *Devil's Bargain* (New York: Penguin Books, 2017), 111.

115 "Exit Polls," *MSNBC*, accessed November 13, 2022.

116 "Pilipinas Debate 2016," YouTube, March 22, 2016, https://www.youtube.com/watch?v=haxzzdIbDR0.

117 Faucheux, *Running for Office*, 157, 158.

118 Katie Dowd, "Here's Who Reportedly Played Trump in Biden's Debate Prep," *SFGATE*, September 29, 2020, https://www.sfgate.com/politics/article/who-played-Trump-in-Biden-debate-prep-15607597.php.

119 Dan Balz, *Collision 2012: Obama vs. Romney and the Future of Elections in America* (New York: Viking, 2013), 309.

120 "Dukakis Lead Widens, According to New Poll," *New York Times*, July 26, 1988, https://www.nytimes.com/1988/07/26/us/dukakis-lead-widens-according-to-new-poll.html.

121 Adam Nahourney, "A Glimmer of Hope for Trump? How Bush Mounted a Comeback in 1988," *New York Times*, August 22, 2020, https://www.nytimes.com/2020/08/22/us/politics/george-bush-comeback-dukakis.html?searchResultPosition=4.

122 "Acceptance Speech / President George H. W. Bush / 1988 Republican National Convention," YouTube, accessed October 27, 2022, https://www.youtube.com/watch?v=gZCwsEozANM.

123 "Acceptance Speech / President George H. W. Bush / 1988 Republican National Convention."

124 Georg Isma, "„Nie hatte ein Kanzlerkandidat weniger Ansehen" : Laschet ist der klare Wahlverlierer, regieren will er trotzdem – im Ernst?" *Tagesspiegel*, September 27, 2021, https://www.tagesspiegel.de/kein-kanzlerkandidat-war-je-so-unbeliebt-laschet-ist-der-klare-wahlverlierer-regieren-will-er-trotzdem--im-ernst-264082.html.

125 "Transcript of John McCain's Concession Speech," *NPR*, November 5, 2008, https://www.npr.org/templates/story/story.php?storyId=96631784.

126 Alan Weiss, "I Don't Remember Asking Your Opinion," website of Alan Weiss, September 22, 2021, https://alanweiss.com/i-dont-remember-asking-your-opinion/.

127 Jill Abramson, "The Nation: Campaign Finance; A Law Survives. Now, Let's Subvert It," *New York Times*, December 14, 2003, https://www.nytimes.com/2003/12/14/weekinreview/the-nation-campaign-finance-a-law-survives-now-let-s-subvert-it.html.

128 Benjamin Siegel and Soo Rin Kim, "Mike Bloomberg Spent More Than $1 Billion on Four-Month Presidential Campaign According to Filing," *ABC News*, April 20, 2020, https://abcnews.go.com/Politics/mike-bloomberg-spent-billion-month-presidential-campaign-filing/story?id=70252435.

129 Fredreka Schouten, "Democrat Jaime Harrison Shatters Senate Fundraising Record in Bid to Oust South Carolina Sen. Lindsey Graham," *CNN*, October 11, 2020, https://edition.cnn.com/2020/10/11/politics/jaime-harrison-fundraising-record-south-carolina-senate-race/index.html.

130 "South Carolina U.S. Senate Election Results," *New York Times*, accessed April 26, 2023, https://www.nytimes.com/interactive/2020/11/03/us/elections/results-south-carolina-senate.html.

131 Amita Kelly, "Biden Announces Record $383 Million September Haul," *NPR*, https://www.npr.org/2020/10/14/923851384/biden-announces-record-383-million-september-haul.

132 Balz, *Collision*, 39.

133 "Am Ende klatschen Moderatoren für Baerbock - doch Interview wird zum Quoten-Reinfall," Focus, April 20, 2021, https://www.focus.de/politik/deutschland/bei-prosieben-am-ende-klatschen-moderatoren-fuer-baerbock-ihr-interview-wird-zum-mega-flop_id_13210704.html.

134 Jade Scipioni, "Michelle Obama: Why Going 'High' When Faced with a Challenge Is So Important to Her," *CNBC*, February 12, 2020, https://www.cnbc.com/2020/02/12/michelle-obama-on-famous-catchphrase-when-they-go-low-we-go-high.html.

135 "Bush Acknowledges 1976 DUI Charge," *CNN*, November 2, 2000, https://edition.cnn.com/2000/ALLPOLITICS/stories/11/02/bush.dui/.

136 Marine Rabreau and Maxime Cuny, "Cinq phrases de Jérôme Cahuzac devenues cultes," *Le Figaro*, February 7, 2016, https://www.lefigaro.fr/economie/le-scan-eco/2016/02/07/29001-20160207ARTFIG00003-cinq-phrases-de-jerome-cahuzac-devenus-cultes.php.

137 "Jérôme Cahuzac condamné en appel à quatre ans de prison dont deux avec sursis," *Midi Libre*, May 15, 2018, https://www.midilibre.fr/2018/05/15/jerome-cahuzac-condamne-en-appel-a-quatre-ans-de-prison-dont-deux-avec-sursis,1671443.php.

138 "Swiftboat Veterans Ad on John Kerry—Any Questions (2004)," YouTube, accessed April 27, 2023, https://www.youtube.com/watch?v=V4Zk9YmED48.

139 "Swift Boat Veterans for Truth," OpenSecrets, accessed April 26, 2023, https://www.opensecrets.org/527s/527events.php?id=61.

140 Perron, *How to Overcome the Power of Incumbency in Election Campaigns*, 137–39.

141 "Trump's uncensored lewd comments about women from 2005," CNN YouTube channel, accessed May 6, 2023, https://www.youtube.com/watch?v=FSC8Q-kR44o.

142 Mark S. Mellman, "Trump's Appeal," in *Campaigning For President 2016*, edited by Dennis Johnson and Lara M. Brown (New York: Routledge, 2018), 96.

143 Peter Schweizer, *Clinton Cash: The Untold Story of How and Why Foreign Governments and Businesses Helped Make Bill and Hillary Rich* (New York: Harper Paperbacks, 2016).

144 "Exit Polls," *MSNBC*, accessed March 19, 2023.

145 Tom Burridge, "Spain Remembers Madrid Train Bombings 10 Years On," *BBC*, March 11, 2014, https://www.bbc.com/news/world-europe-26526704.

146 Alan Weiss, *The Consulting Bible: Everything You Need to Know to Create and Expand a Seven-Figure Consulting Practice* (Hoboken, NJ: John Wiley & Sons, 2011), 70.

147 Branford and Kucinski, *Lula and the Workers Party*, 10.

148 "Rauer Peer und coole Angela: das TV Duell 2013," YouTube, accessed November 5, 2022, https://www.youtube.com/watch?v=qjNG_clZFH4.

149 "Bundestagswahl 2013," Die Bundeswahlleiterin, accessed February 22, 2023, www.bundeswahlleiter.de/bundestagswahlen/2013/ergebnisse/bund-99.html.

150 Gould, *Unfinished Revolution*, 234.

151 Blair, *Journey*, 317.

152 "Vote 2001: Results & Constituencies," *BBC*, accessed February 22, 2023, http://news.bbc.co.uk/hi/english/static/vote2001/results_constituencies/default.stm.

153 Blair, *Journey*, 336.

154 Alan Weiss, *Million Dollar Maverick: Forge Your Own Path to Think Differently, Act Decisively, and Succeed Quickly* (Brookline, MA: Bibliomotion, 2016), 101.

155 Dick Morris, *Power Plays: Win or Lose—How History's Great Political Leaders Play the Game* (New York: Regan Books, 2002), 89–149.

156 Blair, *Journey*, 55, 56.

157 "Das Klima und die Grenzen schützen," *Frankfurter Allgemeine Zeitung*, January 2, 2020, https://www.faz.net/aktuell/politik/ausland/oesterreich-das-klima-und-die-grenzen-schuetzen-16561747.html.

158 Bob Woodward, *The Choice: How Bill Clinton Won* (New York: Simon & Schuster, 1996), 13–23.

159 "Seats in Congress Gained/Lost by the President's Party in Mid-Term Elections," The American Presidency Project, accessed April 27, 2023, https://www.presidency.ucsb.edu/statistics/data/seats-congress-gainedlost-the-presidents-party-mid-term-elections.

160 "Presidential Approval Ratings: Bill Clinton," Gallup, accessed November 5, 2022, https://news.gallup.com/poll/116584/presidential-approval-ratings-bill-clinton.aspx.

161 "The Contract with America: Implementing New Ideas in the U.S.," The Heritage Foundation, accessed October 12, 1995, https://www.heritage.org/political-process/report/the-contract-america-implementing-new-ideas-the-us.

162 Dick Morris, *Behind the Oval Office: Winning the Presidency in the Nineties* (New York: Random House, 1997).

163 Woodward, *Choice*, 26.

164 Woodward, *Choice*, 318–23.

165 Woodward, *Choice*, 211–14.

166 Woodward, *Choice*, 416.

167 Woodward, *Choice*, 236.

168 "The Vote '96," All Politics CNN TIME, accessed February 22, 2023, https://edition.cnn.com/ALLPOLITICS/1996/elections/summary.html.

169 Perron, *How to Overcome the Power of Incumbency in Election Campaigns*, 163–65.

170 Hans-Peter Schwarz, *Helmut Kohl: Eine politische Biographie* (Berlin: Pantheon Verlag, 2012), 753.

171 "5. Parteitag der CDU Deutschlands. Protokoll," Konrad Adenauer Stiftung, accessed February 28, 2023, https://www.kas.de/c/document_library/get_file?uuid=f8687b42-7d73-9c7e-e9d5-e2290057f862&groupId=252038.

172 Schwarz, *Helmut Kohl*, 756, 757.

173 Ursula Feist and Klaus Liepelt, "Demokratie nach Quoten? Zur kommunikationsstrategischen Instrumentalisierung der Wählerforschung im Wahljahr 1994," in *Wahlen und Wähler: Analysen aus Anlass der Bundestagswahl 1994*, edited by Max Kaase and Hans-Dieter Klingemann (Wiesbaden: Springer Fachmedien, 1998), 635.

174 Feist and Liepelt, "Demokratie nach Quoten?", 638.

175 Schwarz, *Helmut Kohl*, 755, 756.

176 Bernhard Weßels, “Wahlpräferenzen in den Regionen: Stabilität und Veränderung im Wahljahr 1994 – oder: Die «Heimkehr» der CDU/CDU-Wähler von 1990,” in *Wahlen und Wähler: Analysen aus Anlass der Bundestagswahl 1994*, edited by Max Kaase and Hans-Dieter Klingemann (Wiesbaden: Springer Fachmedien, 1998), 259–84.

177 “Seats in Congress Gained/Lost by the President’s Party in Mid-Term Elections,” The American Presidency Project, accessed April 29, 2023, https://www.presidency.ucsb.edu/statistics/data/seats-congress-gainedlost-the-presidents-party-mid-term-elections.

178 Balz, *Collision*, 3,4.

179 Balz, *Collision*, 39–41.

180 Balz, *Collision*, 51–56.

181 “Steel,” YouTube, https://www.youtube.com/watch?v=sWiSFwZJXwE.

182 Balz, *Collision*, 57–59.

183 Mark Halperin and John Heilemann, *Double Down: Game Change 2012* (New York: The Penguin Press, 2013), 317–19.

184 “Romney’s Personal Image Remains Negative,” Pew Research Center, August 2, 2012, https://www.pewresearch.org/politics/2012/08/02/romneys-personal-image-remains-negative/.

185 Balz, *Collision*, 261.

186 Halperin and Heilemann, *Double Down*, 332, 333.

187 Author interview with David Plouffe, February 24, 2023.

188 Balz, *Collision*, 257.

189 Halperin and Heilemann, *Double Down*, 331.

190 Author interview with David Plouffe, February 24, 2023.

191 Balz, *Collision*, 75, 76.

192 Roger Simon, “Empty Seats Haunt Obama,” *Politico*, May 8, 2012, https://www.politico.com/story/2012/05/empty-seats-haunt-obama-076017.

193 Balz, *Collision*, 76–79.

194 Balz, *Collision*, 82, 83.

195 Balz, *Collision*, 74–84.

196 “2012,” The American Presidency Project, accessed April 27, 2023, https://www.presidency.ucsb.edu/statistics/elections/2012.

197 Jens Tenscher, “Bundestagswahlkampf 2002—Zwischen strategischem Kalkül und der Inszenierung des Zufalls,” in *Wahlen und Wähler: Analysen aus Anlass der Bundestagswahl 2002*, edited by Jürgen W. Falter, Oscar W. Gabriel, and Bernhard Wessels (Wiesbaden: VS Verlag für Sozialwissenschaften, 2005), 102–33.

198 Tenscher, “Bundestagswahlkampf 2002,” 105.

199 Michael Stürmer, “Als Schröder Stoiber im Hochwasser versenkte,” *WELT*, August 14, 2012, https://www.welt.de/politik/deutschland/article108607179/Als-Schroeder-Stoiber-im-Hochwasser-versenkte.html.

200 Renate Faerber-Husemann, “Als Gerhard Schröder Nein zum Irak-Krieg sagte,” *vorwaerts*, August 2, 2017, https://www.vorwaerts.de/artikel/gerhard-schroeder-irak-krieg-sagte.

201 "Stoiber nennt Schröder einen 'Kronzeugen Saddams'," *Handelsblatt*, September 16, 2002, https://www.handelsblatt.com/archiv/streit-um-irak-politik-eskaliert-stoiber-nennt-schroeder-einen-kronzeugen-saddams/2197276.html.

202 Forschungsgruppe Wahlen, "Zweite Runde für Rot-Grün: Die Bundestagswahl vom 22. September 2002," in *Wahlen und Wähler*, 39, 40.

203 Tenscher, "Bundestagswahlkampf 2002," 111.

204 Jürgen Maier and Thorsten Faas, "Schröder gegen Stoiber: Wahrnehmung, Verarbeitung und Wirkung der Fernsehdebatten im Bundestagswahlkampf 2002," in *Wahlen und Wähler*, 77–101.

205 "Vintage poster, New Labour New Danger, 1997," Conservative Party Shop, accessed April 27, 2023, https://shop.conservatives.com/vintage-poster-new-labour-new-danger-1997.html.

206 Gould, *Unfinished Revolution*, 332–35.

207 Jamieson, *Electing the President*, 118.

INDEX